A Worshipper Always Wins

Living a Life of Victorious Worship

Gerard Assey

A Worshipper Always Wins

Living a Life of Victorious Worship

By

Gerard Assey

Published by:

Gerard Assey

19/18, Palli Arasan Street

Anna Nagar East

Chennai - 600 102

ISBN: 978-81-986974-6-2

Table of Contents

Disclaimer:

Any resemblance (names, characters, and scenarios used in this book, including testimonies and personal stories) to actual persons, living or dead, or actual events is purely coincidental. These examples are used solely for illustrative and teaching purposes.

The intent is to inspire and equip readers, not to depict real individuals or specific events. No harm or misrepresentation is intended.

Introduction: The Unchanging Truth

Why Worship is Central to Victory

Worship is not merely an activity—it is a posture, a position, and a weapon. In every generation, culture, and crisis, those who have chosen to bow before God in authentic worship have stood up victorious in life's battles. Worship is the believer's response to the greatness of God, and that response activates heaven's intervention on earth.

From the beginning of time, worship has been the dividing line between defeat and deliverance. It was not weaponry, wealth, or worldly wisdom that led ancient armies to triumph; it was often the sound of surrendered hearts lifted in praise. Worship aligns the worshipper with God's will, power, and presence, positioning them to receive divine instruction, protection, and provision. In short, a worshipper does not fight for victory—he fights from victory.

Consider King Jehoshaphat in 2 Chronicles 20. Facing an alliance of powerful enemies, he did not arm his strongest warriors first—he positioned the worshippers ahead of the army. Their song was not of strategy or strength, but of surrender: *"Give thanks to the Lord, for His love endures forever."* And as they worshipped, God set ambushes against their enemies. Worship became their battlefield.

Victory doesn't always come in the form of visible success or instant results, but a worshipper knows that victory is the peace within, the clarity of mind, and the confidence that God is in control—regardless of the circumstance. Worship is central to victory because it makes God central to the battle.

The Worshipper's Secret Weapon

Many believers live as if worship is an optional part of the Christian life—something to be done on Sundays, or only when life is smooth. But for the true worshipper, worship is a spiritual weapon, sharper than any sword and more effective than any strategy. Worship breaks chains that prayer alone may not. It softens hardened hearts. It confuses the enemy. Worship, especially when offered in the valley, becomes an act of war against despair, fear, and darkness.

Paul and Silas understood this secret. In Acts 16, they were wrongly imprisoned, beaten, and bound. Yet, they did not complain or curse their captors. Instead, they lifted their voices in worship—singing hymns at midnight. That moment shifted everything. The prison doors flung open, not just for them but for all prisoners around them. Their worship unlocked a divine response that no human effort could manufacture.

This is the secret: worship turns your prison into a platform, your pain into power, and your waiting into a witness. It invites God to do what only He can do.

Worship as a Lifestyle, Not an Event

Modern-day Christianity often reduces worship to a church service or a song. But worship, in its truest form, is a life laid down. It is Abraham, willing to offer his son (Genesis 22). It is the widow of Zarephath, giving her last meal to Elijah (1 Kings 17). It is Mary, pouring expensive perfume on Jesus' feet (John 12). Worship is not just about lifting hands in a song—it is about lifting your life in surrender.

Let us meet Anaya, a school teacher in a small town in Kerala, India. She was diagnosed with a degenerative eye condition that threatened to take her vision. Yet, instead of despairing, she began each day in worship—thanking God for every ray of light she could still see. Her students noticed her joy, even as her condition worsened. She never once asked, *"Why me?"* Instead, she declared, *"Even if I cannot see with my eyes, I will always see with my spirit."* Years later, though legally blind, Anaya continues to teach—now using audio tools—and her story has drawn many to Christ. Her life is worship, not just her words.

Living a lifestyle of worship means you respond to both mountain and valley with the same heart—one that trusts, praises, and surrenders. It's giving your best even when you feel your worst. It's forgiving when it hurts. It's choosing obedience over convenience. That kind of life may not be celebrated by the world, but it is crowned by heaven.

Distinction between Praise and Worship

While praise and worship are often used interchangeably, they are distinctly different yet powerfully connected.

Praise is the joyful recounting of all God has done. It is expressive, external, and often loud. Praise can happen even when you don't feel spiritually deep—it is about acknowledging God's acts. Psalm 100:4 says, *"Enter His gates with thanksgiving and His courts with praise."* Praise is the doorway into deeper communion with God.

Worship, however, goes further. Worship is intimate and internal—it is the heart bowing before God for who He is, not just what He has done. It is recognizing His holiness, majesty, and worthiness. Worship requires the whole self: heart, mind, body, and soul. It is deeper, quieter, and more sacrificial. Where praise may be easy in good times, worship endures through the fire.

Take for example Jared, a 45-year-old marketing executive from Nairobi. He lost his job in a downsizing effort. With bills piling up, he felt tempted to panic. But instead of succumbing to anxiety, Jared shut himself in his room, lifted his hands, and whispered, *"God, even without a job, You are still my Provider."* That night, he slept peacefully for the first time in weeks. Two weeks later, he was offered a better role, one that aligned with his passion and values. Jared's shift from praise (for blessings) to worship (for God's character) unlocked a door no résumé could.

True victory comes not just when we praise God for His gifts but when we worship Him for who He is—*unchanging, faithful, and sovereign*.

Introduction to the Central Scripture Theme

The thread that runs through this book is simple but profound: **A worshipper always wins**. Not because life is without trial, but because God always honors those who honor Him.

Consider these foundational scriptures:

- ✓ **2 Chronicles 20:21-22**

  "As they began to sing and praise, the Lord set ambushes against the men... and they were defeated."

  Worshippers led the army, and God responded by defeating the enemies. Victory began with a song, not a sword.

- ✓ **John 4:23-24**
  "Yet a time is coming and has now come when the true worshippers will worship the Father in spirit and truth..."
  Jesus identifies the kind of worship the Father seeks. Not religious ritual, but sincere surrender. Worship is not limited by geography, denomination, or tradition—it is spirit and truth.
- ✓ **Acts 16:25-26**
  "About midnight Paul and Silas were praying and singing hymns to God... and suddenly there was such a violent earthquake..."
  From chains to freedom, from prison to purpose—worship became the catalyst for the miraculous.

These are not isolated incidents; they are eternal principles. Worship shifts the natural by aligning it with the supernatural. Every time someone in Scripture worshipped in the midst of hardship, confusion, or danger, God responded—with deliverance, breakthrough, or peace.

And today, the same God is still responding to the sound of worship.

Worship as the Eternal Key

Worship is not outdated. It's not optional. It's not decorative. It's the eternal key to God's presence and power. Heaven is filled with worship—angels cry "Holy," elders cast crowns, and multitudes sing. If worship is the sound of heaven, it must be the lifestyle of those who belong to heaven's King.

Victory begins—not when the situation changes—but when your heart changes toward God through worship. This book will take you on a journey: from understanding to application, from head knowledge to heart surrender. Because one truth remains unchanging: **A worshipper always wins.**

PART I:
THE FOUNDATION OF VICTORIOUS WORSHIP

Chapter 1:
The Origin of Worship

Worship in Heaven before Creation

Before time began, before the foundation of the earth was laid, before the sun ever shone or rivers flowed, there was worship. Worship is not a product of religion—it is the eternal activity of heaven and the heartbeat of creation. Long before mankind ever sang a song or lifted hands in surrender, the heavenly realms echoed with adoration for the Most High God.

Ezekiel 28:12-17 paints a stunning portrait of Lucifer, the anointed cherub who once stood in splendor and perfection in heaven. He wasn't just a worshipper—he was created *for* worship. Covered in precious stones and equipped with built-in instruments, Lucifer embodied the beauty of musical worship. The Bible says, *"The workmanship of your timbrels and pipes was prepared for you on the day you were created"* (Ezekiel 28:13). Worship was not just his role; it was his essence.

But then came pride.

Isaiah 14:12-15 reveals Lucifer's fatal ambition*: "I will ascend to heaven; I will raise my throne above the stars of God…"* Instead of directing worship to God, he desired to redirect it to himself. Worship, meant to reflect God's glory, became hijacked by a lust for personal exaltation. This rebellion fractured heaven. Lucifer was cast down, and with him, a third of the angels who joined his mutiny.

This origin story is vital. It teaches us that true worship is about God's glory, not ours. It reminds us that worship becomes corrupted when the worshipper seeks the spotlight. What once resided in perfection was torn apart by pride. This heavenly history sets the tone for everything that would follow on Earth. Worship began in heaven, and its battle continues today—between the pure-hearted worshipper and the self-seeking performer.

The First Act of Worship on Earth

The story of worship on earth begins in the early chapters of Genesis, not with words, but with actions. Genesis 4 introduces us to two brothers—Cain and Abel, both bringing offerings to God. This moment is one of the most profound in Scripture, not because of what they brought, but because of the posture behind it.

Abel brought the best portions of the firstborn of his flock, while Cain offered some of the fruits of the soil. Scripture tells us plainly: *"The Lord looked with favor on Abel and his offering, but on Cain and his offering He did not look with favor"* (Genesis 4:4-5). Why the difference? It wasn't about livestock versus crops—it was about heart posture.

Hebrews 11:4 confirms this: *"By faith Abel brought God a better offering than Cain did."* Abel's act was rooted in faith, reverence, and gratitude. Cain's offering, though outwardly acceptable, lacked the inward substance of surrender.

And here, the earth learns its first painful lesson: worship that pleases God must come from the heart, not just the hands.

This moment led to envy, then murder, as Cain slew his brother. Worship, when corrupted or misunderstood, can breed resentment. The altar, which should unite, became the scene of division. Yet, even in this tragic beginning, God was teaching mankind: Worship is not about ritual—it's about relationship.

The First Mention of "Worship" in the Bible

While acts of worship occurred earlier, the first time the word *"worship"* is actually used in Scripture is in Genesis 22. And what a moment it is.

Abraham, the father of faith, is tested in the deepest way possible. God asks him to sacrifice his promised son, Isaac—the very child through whom God had vowed to establish a great nation. With a heavy heart and unwavering obedience, Abraham journeys to Mount Moriah.

When he sees the mountain from afar, he says to his servants, *"Stay here… while I and the boy go over there. We will worship and then we will come back to you."* (Genesis 22:5)

This is the first recorded use of the word "worship." *Notice what Abraham does not say. He does not say,* "We're going to sing," or *"We're going to pray."* He says, "We will worship."

In Abraham's heart, worship meant surrender—a willingness to lay down what he loved most in obedience to God.

Of course, we know how the story ends. Just as Abraham lifts the knife, God intervenes. A ram is caught in the thicket, and Isaac's life is spared. But the message is clear: worship is costly. It requires trust. And it always results in God's provision.

To this day, Mount Moriah remains a holy site—not because of a song sung or incense burned, but because of a father's surrendered heart. True worship, the kind that moves heaven, looks like Abraham's—obedient, sacrificial, and rooted in faith.

The Echo of Worship Through Lives Today

Let's fast-forward to today, into the life of Leah, a 33-year-old nurse in the outskirts of Kampala, Uganda. She had always been close to her mother, a widow who raised her alone after her father died when she was five. When her mother was diagnosed with terminal cancer, Leah was devastated. She prayed for healing, fasted, and believed. But her mother passed away just three months later.

Friends expected Leah to turn away from God in anger. But at the funeral, Leah stood up to speak. Her voice cracked with emotion as she said, *"I do not understand why God chose this path, but I trust Him. I will still worship."* And then she sang a quiet hymn her mother had loved.

Leah's life became a reflection of Abraham's worship—not about feelings, not about outcomes, but about surrender.

Months later, a young patient heard Leah singing the same hymn in the hospital. He asked about the song, and through that conversation, he came to know Christ. Worship continues to ripple through Leah's life—not just through song, but through surrender, just like Abraham.

Worship as Heaven's Original Language

From the halls of heaven to the hills of Moriah, from the flawed offering of Cain to the faith-filled sacrifice of Abraham, worship has been humanity's deepest expression of love and dependence on God. It is not an invention of religion, but the very language of creation—taught by angels, marred by pride, redeemed through surrender.

Lucifer's fall reminds us that worship is not about talent—it's about truth. Cain's offering warns us that worship is not about activity—it's about attitude. And Abraham's obedience shows us that worship is not about convenience—it's about costly surrender.

In every era and every soul, the origin of worship points us to one unchanging truth: God desires hearts, not habits. Worship that brings victory always begins in surrender.

Chapter 2: Why Worship Matters to God

In the grand drama of human history, few themes echo louder in the heart of God than worship. It's not just a religious activity or a set of rituals; it's a divine invitation into intimacy. Worship matters to God not because He needs affirmation, but because He desires connection. He seeks not mechanical praise, but meaningful presence. From Eden to eternity, from the tabernacle to the upper room, worship is God's call to communion, not performance.

God's Desire for Relationship Over Religion (John 4:23–24)

In one of the most profound conversations recorded in the Bible, Jesus meets a Samaritan woman at Jacob's well (John 4). She is a woman marked by brokenness—five husbands behind her, and now living with a man who is not her husband. Socially marginalized, religiously confused, and emotionally weary, she comes to the well seeking water but finds living truth.

Their dialogue shifts quickly to worship. She raises the long-standing debate between Jews and Samaritans: *"Our ancestors worshiped on this mountain, but you Jews claim that the place where we must worship is in Jerusalem."* (John 4:20)

But Jesus doesn't get drawn into a location-based argument. Instead, He makes a declaration that reshaped the understanding of worship forever:

"Yet a time is coming and has now come when the true worshipers will worship the Father in spirit and truth, for they are the kind of worshipers the Father

seeks. God is spirit, and His worshipers must worship in the Spirit and in truth." (John 4:23–24)

God seeks worshipers. Not rituals. Not traditions. Not empty religion. Worship matters to God because it is the language of relationship, not regulation.

In this moment, Jesus shows us that worship is not confined to sacred spaces or special seasons. It's not about buildings or backgrounds—it's about the heart. True worship connects spirit to Spirit, heart to heart. The Father longs for intimacy, not idolatry; connection, not custom.

And so, in a dusty village of Samaria, with no choir, no instruments, and no religious ceremony, worship is redefined—not as something we perform, but as someone we become.

God Inhabits the Praises of His People (Psalm 22:3)

David, the man after God's heart, pens one of the most heart-wrenching psalms ever written—Psalm 22. It begins with anguish:

"My God, my God, why have You forsaken me?"—words Jesus Himself would echo on the cross.

But hidden within this cry of abandonment is a powerful truth in verse 3: *"Yet You are holy, enthroned on the praises of Israel."* (Psalm 22:3)

This means that God dwells, abides, lives in the praises of His people. Where praise rises, God descends. Where worship is lifted, Heaven aligns with earth. Worship, then, is more than just admiration—it is a throne-building activity. Every time we praise, we build a space for His presence to reign.

When King Jehoshaphat faced the terrifying armies of Moab and Ammon (2 Chronicles 20), he did something humanly absurd—he appointed singers to go before the army. They sang, *"Give thanks to the Lord, for His love endures forever."* And as they worshiped, God sent ambushes against their enemies. Worship built God a throne in the battle—and He ruled from it.

This is why worship matters: it attracts His presence. And wherever He is present, victory follows.

Worship as Surrender and Alignment with Heaven

In its purest form, worship is surrender. It is the posture of the heart that says, *"Not my will, but Yours be done."* It's the spiritual act of bowing low even when circumstances shout loud. It is alignment—not of emotion, but of authority. When we worship, we are saying to Heaven, *"You are Lord, and I am not. Take Your place."*

This was the lesson Job lived. Stripped of his wealth, children, and health, he faced the ultimate test. And what did he do?

"Then Job arose, tore his robe, shaved his head, and fell to the ground and worshiped. He said: 'Naked I came from my mother's womb, and naked I will depart. The Lord gave and the Lord has taken away; blessed be the name of the Lord.'" (Job 1:20–21)

In pain, he worshiped.

In confusion, he surrendered.

In loss, he aligned himself with Heaven's sovereignty.

That is worship—not sanitized, not cheerful—but raw, real, reverent. Job didn't worship because life was good; he worshiped because God is good. Even when he didn't understand, he trusted. This kind of worship shakes hell and moves heaven.

Real Life: A Story of Surrendered Worship

Meet Marcus, a 47-year-old real estate consultant in Atlanta. He once lived for success—multi-million-dollar contracts, cars, recognition, and the pride of achievement. A self-made man. Church was a Sunday checkbox. Worship? A couple of hands raised to "get in the mood."

But in one season, everything collapsed. A failed business deal led to a domino effect of lawsuits, a strained marriage, and the eventual loss of his home. With two children to feed and his pride shattered, Marcus sat in the corner of a shelter one evening, holding a cold cup of coffee.

That night, a local worship team came to serve dinner and sing a few songs. A young woman began to sing softly: *"You are good, good, oh…"*

Something broke inside Marcus. He dropped the cup and wept uncontrollably. That night, he didn't sing to feel better—he surrendered. In a broken voice, he began to speak, *"Lord, if all I have is You, You are still enough. Take what's left."*

From that night onward, Marcus changed. His circumstances didn't improve overnight, but something deeper shifted. He became a man of worship. Daily, in the park, in borrowed clothes, he lifted his hands—not for applause, but in alignment.

Two years later, Marcus now runs a small home-repair business and mentors men coming out of homelessness. Worship wasn't a moment for him—it became a new life rhythm. And in that rhythm, God rebuilt him, piece by piece. Worship brought him back into alignment with Heaven—and there, he found victory.

Why Worship Matters to God: A Father's Heart

So why does worship matter so deeply to God?

Because it is the one thing He seeks (John 4:23). It's not because He lacks love or admiration—but because worship is the meeting point between His heart and ours.

Worship says: *"I trust You, even when I don't understand."*

Worship says: *"I choose You above all else."*

Worship says: *"You reign, even in my ruins."*

More than songs, more than rituals, God desires hearts that know Him, respond to Him, and remain surrendered to Him.

When we worship, we become the very thing we were created to be: image-bearers in communion with our Creator.

Closing Reflection

Worship is not a musical interlude in our lives; it is the lifeblood of our relationship with God. It matters to Him not because it flatters Him—but because it forms us. It brings Heaven's order into our chaos. It builds a throne for His presence. It releases peace in pain. And most importantly, it fulfills the longing of the Father's heart—to walk with His children in spirit and in truth.

Worship is Heaven's welcome mat. And every time we lay down our pride, our plans, our pain, or our positions, we step into the very presence of the One who never fails.

Chapter 3: The Worship-Win Principle in the Bible

From Genesis to Revelation, a divine pattern unfolds—worship is a weapon of victory. Worship is not merely expressive; it is explosive. It is not just the prelude to spiritual battle; often, it **is** the battle. Worship precedes breakthrough, precedes deliverance, precedes conquest. This truth is echoed across the tapestry of Scripture and throughout the lives of those who dared to exalt God in their lowest, most uncertain, or most fearful moments.

The Worship-Win Principle is simple but profound: When worship goes up, God comes down—and where God dwells, victory is inevitable.

The Pattern of Victory Through Worship

Let us journey again back to the time of King Jehoshaphat, the ruler of Judah, as recorded in 2 Chronicles 20. News arrives that a vast army—Moabites, Ammonites, and others—are coming against him. The nation is outnumbered, unprepared, and facing annihilation.

Jehoshaphat does what many leaders fail to do—he admits his fear and seeks God. He calls for a national fast, and the people assemble. In his prayer, Jehoshaphat acknowledges God's sovereignty: *"We do not know what to do, but our eyes are on You."* (2 Chronicles 20:12)

Then comes a prophetic word from Jahaziel: *"Do not be afraid or discouraged because of this vast army. For the battle is not yours, but God's... Take up your positions; stand firm and see the deliverance the Lord will give you."* (2 Chronicles 20:15-17)

Jehoshaphat believes—and then does something unthinkable. He appoints singers to go ahead of the army, praising the Lord with the words: *"Give thanks to the Lord, for His love endures forever."*

As they began to sing and praise, God set ambushes against their enemies, and they were defeated without Judah lifting a sword.

This is the Worship-Win Principle in action. Worship was not the response to the victory—it was the reason for the victory.

God fights for worshipers. He responds not just to the noise, but to the posture of trust that worship declares.

How God Fights for Worshipers

The story of Paul and Silas in Acts 16 is another powerful testimony. Wrongfully arrested, beaten, and shackled in a Philippian prison, they faced a night of humiliation and hopelessness. Yet at midnight, they didn't grumble or beg—they worshiped.

"About midnight Paul and Silas were praying and singing hymns to God, and the other prisoners were listening to them." (Acts 16:25)

Then came the miracle.

"Suddenly there was such a violent earthquake that the foundations of the prison were shaken. At once all the prison doors flew open, and everyone's chains came loose." (Acts 16:26)

Worship shook the foundations. Worship broke chains. Worship opened doors. But the real victory wasn't just physical—it was spiritual. The jailer and his entire household were saved.

When we worship in the darkness, God fights in the light. When we lift our hands, He lifts His sword.

Worship Shifts the Atmosphere (Spiritual Laws of Worship)

There is a spiritual law that governs the dynamics of worship—where God is exalted, Satan is dethroned.

In the unseen realm, worship is more than melody—it is warfare. It brings divine order, heavenly clarity, and the rule of God into chaotic circumstances.

This is seen in the life of David, the shepherd boy turned king. In 1 Samuel 16:23, when King Saul was tormented by an evil spirit, David was summoned to play the harp. As he worshiped, the demonic influence departed.

"Whenever the spirit from God came on Saul, David would take up his harp and play. Then relief would come to Saul; he would feel better, and the evil spirit would leave him."

David didn't preach. He didn't confront the spirit. He simply worshiped—and the atmosphere shifted.

This same law still operates today. Where true worship is lifted, heaven invades earth. Demonic oppression, confusion, anxiety, and despair cannot cohabit with God's manifest presence. Worship displaces darkness and enthrones God.

Real Life: Carla's Atmosphere Shift

Carla Thompson, a 38-year-old high school teacher from Durham, North Carolina, had always believed in God but never truly practiced worship. Life had grown heavy—divorce, a rebellious teenage son, and the recent diagnosis of breast cancer had driven her into depression. She stopped attending church. Prayer felt empty. Life had no music.

One night, unable to sleep, Carla turned on her old laptop and clicked on a forgotten folder marked "Church Songs." As the soft strains of *"Way Maker"* filled the room, something happened. She began to weep. Her hands trembled as she lifted them, whispering, *"Lord, I can't do this anymore… I give it to You."*

From that moment, Carla began a new daily rhythm. Before checking her phone, before the medical updates or the stress of parenting—she worshiped. Alone, in her room, voice cracking, body trembling—she chose to exalt God above her storm.

Within three months, something changed. Not the diagnosis—but the atmosphere. Her son, without prompting, began to attend church with her. Her oncologist noticed unexpected shrinkage in the tumor. Her smile returned.

She didn't worship to manipulate God—she worshiped to magnify Him. And in doing so, she shifted the atmosphere of her soul. Carla is now cancer-free, but she says her real healing happened before the tumor left—when worship entered.

Worship Always Wins

The Worship-Win Principle is not just a biblical pattern—it is a spiritual law. When we worship, we declare:

God is King, even when life feels out of control.

God is good, even when things are hard.

God is fighting, even when we cannot see it.

Worship is not the absence of battle—it is the announcement of victory.

Jehoshaphat worshiped—and the enemy was confused.

Paul and Silas worshiped—and the prison shook.

David worshiped—and torment fled.
Carla worshiped—and her world changed.
This is why worship is not optional—it is vital. It is not an emotional filler—it is a spiritual force. Heaven moves when God is exalted. And when heaven moves, nothing remains the same.
Worship always wins—not because it changes God, but because it changes everything around Him.

PART II:

VICTORIES THROUGH WORSHIP – BIBLICAL CASE STUDIES

Chapter 4: Jehoshaphat – Worshippers on the Battlefield

It is often in our most impossible battles that God reveals His most unusual strategies. Sometimes, when the enemy is closing in, and fear threatens to drown faith, God's instructions seem illogical—irrational even. Yet, in those very moments, heaven's power is released when earth obeys without question. This is the heart of the story of King Jehoshaphat, whose decision to place singers in front of soldiers redefined the rules of war and carved into history one of the most astounding victories ever recorded.

The Crisis in Judah

The scene in 2 Chronicles 20 opens with impending disaster. The Moabites, Ammonites, and Meunites—a vast coalition—had joined forces and were marching toward Judah. Word reached Jehoshaphat that a "great multitude" was advancing rapidly. The text says, *"Jehoshaphat was afraid and set himself to seek the Lord"* (v. 3). This fear, though real, drove him in the right direction—toward God, not away from Him.

A nationwide fast was declared, and the people of Judah gathered to seek help from the Lord. Standing before them at the temple courtyard, Jehoshaphat cried out to God. His prayer was not one of panic but one grounded in the memory of God's past faithfulness and a confession of human helplessness:

"We do not know what to do, but our eyes are on You." (2 Chronicles 20:12)

That confession wasn't weakness—it was worship. It was the posture of a man who knew that the battle before him required more than military strength; it required divine intervention.

Then came the word of the Lord through a Levite named Jahaziel:

"Do not be afraid or discouraged because of this vast army. For the battle is not yours, but God's." (v. 15)

What followed was a strategy that could never have been birthed in a war room.

Worship as a Weapon

The next morning, Jehoshaphat prepared the people—not for hand-to-hand combat, but for worship. Instead of placing the strongest warriors at the front lines, he appointed singers to go before the army, declaring:

"Give thanks to the Lord, for His steadfast love endures forever." (v. 21)

It defies every military principle ever known: to fight an army with music, to face swords with songs.

And yet, as the voices of praise rose, something inexplicable happened:

"The Lord set ambushes against the men of Ammon and Moab and Mount Seir who were invading Judah, and they were defeated." (v. 22)

The enemy armies turned on one another. By the time the people of Judah arrived at the battlefield, they found only corpses—not one enemy soldier had survived.

Praise had confused the enemy. Worship won the war.

The Faith-Action Dynamic

Jehoshaphat did not sit idle waiting for God to act. His worship was not passive; it was a faith-filled action. He aligned his people not just with God's words, but with God's ways.

The victory came when they combined obedience to God's command with faithful worship, even before seeing the outcome. This is the same faith-action dynamic that is echoed throughout Scripture:

- ✓ Noah built an ark before rain ever fell.
- ✓ Abraham raised a knife over Isaac before God provided a ram.
- ✓ Joshua marched around Jericho before a single brick fell.

In all of these, worship preceded manifestation. It is in trusting obedience that heaven releases its power.

Modern Echo: The Story of Darius Emmanuel

In the outskirts of Accra, Ghana, Darius Emmanuel, a 42-year-old worship leader, found himself in his own Jehoshaphat moment. A faithful servant in his local church, Darius had built a small Christian school from the ground up to educate underprivileged children. He funded it from his earnings, often sacrificing his own needs to pay for books, uniforms, and teachers' salaries.

But one day, a land dispute emerged. A wealthy businessman, backed by corrupt local officials, claimed the property. A court order was issued: vacate in 14 days or the building would be demolished.

Darius was devastated. His appeals were ignored. His bank accounts were frozen due to legal complications. He wept. He fasted. And then—he worshiped.

On the final Sunday before the deadline, he gathered his students, teachers, and church members on the school ground. With guitars, drums, and tear-streaked faces, they sang:

"This is how I fight my battles… It may look like I'm surrounded, but I'm surrounded by You."

Neighbors came out to watch. Some mocked. Others wept.

The next morning, as bulldozers arrived, something remarkable happened. The businessman was arrested on unrelated fraud charges overnight. The case was reopened. Within weeks, the court ruled in Darius's favor.

Darius would later say: *"I did not worship for a miracle. I worshiped because I had nothing else but God. And in that moment, He was enough."*

Darius, like Jehoshaphat, discovered that God doesn't just respond to worship—He inhabits it. And where God abides, the enemy is scattered.

The Mystery and Majesty of Worship in Warfare

Worship is not denial. Jehoshaphat saw the armies. Darius knew the bulldozers were coming. Worship doesn't ignore the problem; it exalts the Problem-Solver above the problem. When we worship, we confess that God is bigger than our enemies, our fear, our circumstances.

It is not sound that confuses the enemy—it is the substance of faith behind the sound.

Satan, the prince of confusion, becomes confused when he hears a child of God singing in the storm. He cannot understand joy in pain, peace in persecution, or thanksgiving in crisis. Worship disorients the demonic.

The Battlefield Belongs to Worshippers

The story of Jehoshaphat is not a historical anomaly—it is a spiritual template. When we face overwhelming odds, we must remember:

- ✓ The battle is not ours, but the Lord's.
- ✓ Worship is not the song of the victorious; it is the strategy for victory.
- ✓ Faith is not just felt; it is demonstrated in obedience, even when the odds say otherwise.

As believers, we do not fight for victory—we fight from victory. The weapon in our hand is not always a sword; sometimes, it is a song.

So when the enemy surrounds, lift your voice. When the battle feels impossible, lift your hands. When fear whispers defeat, raise your praise.

For worship is not what we do after we win. Worship is how we win.

Chapter 5: Paul & Silas – Prison Breakthrough through Praise

There are moments in life when everything seems to cave in—when hope appears buried under the weight of suffering, injustice, and fear. It's in those moments, not on mountaintops but in valleys, not in daylight but at midnight, that the true essence of worship is revealed. Worship, in its purest form, is not born in comfort. It is forged in the fire of adversity. Nowhere is this more evident than in the dim prison cell where Paul and Silas chose to sing instead of scream, praise instead of panic.

The Setting: A Prison for Preaching

In Acts 16, Paul and Silas were on a missionary journey in Philippi. Their ministry was fruitful—lives were being changed. However, their deliverance of a young slave girl who was possessed with a spirit of divination stirred the wrath of her exploiters. They had no interest in the girl's healing; her value lay in her profitability.

As a result, Paul and Silas were dragged before the magistrates, falsely accused, severely beaten, and thrown into prison. Their feet were fastened in stocks—immobilized, their backs bloodied from rods, their reputation tarnished, and their freedom stolen.

They had every reason to lament. Every justification to retreat into silence. But instead, they chose worship.

"About midnight, Paul and Silas were praying and singing hymns to God, and the other prisoners were listening to them." (Acts 16:25)
Midnight—not just a time of the day, but a metaphor for despair. The point of deepest darkness. Yet it was in that hour that a sound rose—an act of defiance against the spirit of discouragement.
They didn't sing after the miracle. They sang before it.

The Power of Praise in Darkness
There's something supernatural about praising God when it hurts. Worship in pain declares that God is worthy, not because of what He does, but because of who He is. That kind of worship rattles the foundations of spiritual prisons.
Paul and Silas' song was not for show—it was an act of trust. They were not singing for a miracle; they were singing because they knew God was still in control, whether they were freed or not.
But heaven heard their praise.
"Suddenly there was a great earthquake, so that the foundations of the prison were shaken. And immediately all the doors were opened, and everyone's bonds were unfastened." (Acts 16:26)
It wasn't just their chains that fell. Every prisoner in that jail experienced the collateral impact of worship. Freedom didn't come through human effort—it came through divine response to praise.
What's striking is that Paul and Silas didn't even try to escape. They stayed put. Because their goal wasn't just personal deliverance—it was divine presence.
The jailer, about to kill himself, stopped when Paul called out. This man who once bound them would

soon be bowing with them. He and his entire household were saved that night. Worship didn't just bring freedom; it brought transformation.

The Modern Echo: Emilia Rosario's Midnight Song

In the heart of Mexico City lived Emilia Rosario, a single mother of two and a trained classical violinist who had once played in the national symphony. But after her husband abandoned the family and mounting bills forced her to leave the orchestra, Emilia found herself cleaning houses to make ends meet. She clung to God, but life had bruised her soul.

One evening, her youngest child, Sofia, developed a high fever. Emilia rushed her to the hospital, only to be told that Sofia needed medication that Emilia could not afford. As she sat in the hospital corridor holding her daughter, hopelessness consumed her like a rising tide.

It was past midnight. She had no solutions, no savings, and no strength. But she had her violin.

She opened the old case. With trembling fingers, she began to play softly in the hospital hallway. She played the old hymn, *"Great is Thy Faithfulness."* Tears poured down her cheeks—not of sorrow, but of surrender.

Doctors paused. Nurses gathered. Strangers listened. One elderly man stepped forward, placed a hand on Emilia's shoulder, and said, *"I don't know what your need is, but the Lord told me to cover it. Completely."*

Sofia was treated. She recovered fully. That man turned out to be a retired doctor and Christian

philanthropist who later helped Emilia establish a music school for underprivileged youth.
Emilia later said, *"That night I didn't play to change my situation. I played because I refused to let the darkness steal my song. And God met me in the hallway."*
Like Paul and Silas, Emilia worshipped in her darkest hour—and heaven responded.

When Worship Becomes Warfare
What happened in that Philippian jail and in that hospital corridor is not a myth. It's the spiritual law of worship. When we lift our voice in surrender, even while shackled by circumstance, we release the presence of God into the environment.

- ✓ Worship shifts atmospheres. It doesn't deny the chains, but it invokes a reality greater than the chains.
- ✓ Worship at midnight releases light.
- ✓ Worship in prison opens doors.
- ✓ Worship in pain becomes prophecy.

The enemy wants silence in your suffering. But heaven invites a song. Why? Because when worship rises from broken places, it becomes a weapon—not against flesh and blood, but against principalities and powers.

Praise in the Prison Is the Key
What if Paul and Silas had stayed silent? What if Emilia had packed her violin away? What if your current valley is an invitation for breakthrough—but it must be accessed through praise?
The kind of praise that is born not in outcomes but in unshaken faith. The kind that sings not *because* of freedom, but *until* freedom.

Friend, maybe your midnight hour is now. Maybe the stocks around your feet are not iron, but anxiety, debt, betrayal, or grief. And perhaps what God is waiting for is not your plan, but your praise.
Because praise at midnight isn't denial—it's defiance.
A declaration that even in the dark, God is good.
Lift your song. Shake the prison. Someone else's freedom may depend on the sound you release.

Chapter 6:
Joshua and the Fall of Jericho – Obedient Worship

Some walls fall with hammers. Others collapse with time. But the walls of Jericho—fortified, proud, and ancient—fell at the sound of obedient worship.

Obedient worship may not always make sense to the human mind, but in the kingdom of God, obedience is one of the most powerful expressions of worship. This truth stands boldly in the account of Joshua and the conquest of Jericho. Their victory was not the result of military brilliance but of unquestioning obedience to a divine command that defied logic.

The Setting: A Wall Too Thick to Breach

Jericho was the gateway to the Promised Land. To take Canaan, the Israelites had to conquer Jericho. The city was tightly shut—no one went in or came out. Its walls were so thick that history records chariots could ride across them. In human terms, it was impenetrable.

Joshua, having just taken over leadership from Moses, now stood on the edge of promise and impossibility. But God spoke.

"See, I have delivered Jericho into your hands, along with its king and its fighting men." (Joshua 6:2)

It's remarkable. God said, *"I have delivered,"* even though nothing had yet changed physically. To God, the battle was already won. What remained was Israel's obedient response to His unconventional instruction.

March. Don't fight. Walk in silence. Then blow trumpets.

To a warrior, it sounded absurd. To a worshipper, it was an invitation.

Joshua obeyed.

For six days, the Israelites marched once around the city in silence, just as the Lord had said. On the seventh day, they marched seven times, and on the seventh lap, the priests blew the trumpets, and the people gave a shout—not a shout of frustration or fear, but a shout of faith. And the walls collapsed.

No stones thrown. No swords raised. Worship in the form of obedience brought the victory.

Obedience as Worship

In our culture, worship is often seen as music or liturgy, but biblically, worship is deeper—it is surrender. It is trust expressed through action. In Joshua's case, worship meant doing something that made no strategic sense—yet trusting God over his instincts.

Why did the walls fall?

Because the people chose to obey. And their obedience became the sound of faith. It wasn't just the trumpet. It was the combination of silence, persistence, process, and finally, praise at the appointed time that shook the foundations.

Obedient worship does not always yield instant results. It requires patience and perseverance. The Israelites had to show up every day, circle the city, say nothing, and trust that God was working behind the scenes.

The Modern Echo: Malik's March Around Fear

Malik Thompson was a high school football coach in rural Georgia, known for his discipline and passion for mentoring young men. His life was turned upside down when he was wrongfully accused of misconduct by a vengeful parent after he benched the parent's son for unsportsmanlike behavior.

Though the charges were baseless, the scandal spread fast. Malik was suspended, his reputation shattered. Every media outlet painted him in the worst light. His dream career teetered on collapse.

While his lawyer advised damage control and PR statements, Malik sensed the Lord leading him to silence. *"Don't fight this in the court of public opinion,"* the Spirit whispered. *"Walk with Me."*

Instead of defending himself publicly, Malik began walking around his old high school football field every morning before sunrise. He prayed. He worshipped. He obeyed. Seven weeks passed—his own Jericho march.

One day, the parent who had made the accusations came forward with a tearful confession. Overwhelmed by guilt and unable to sleep, he told the truth to school authorities and the media. Malik was cleared of all charges.

But that wasn't the end.

When the truth came out, the school board not only reinstated him—they promoted him to athletic director. And the same community that once judged him, now stood and applauded when he returned to the field.

"I didn't win by shouting back," Malik told his players later. *"I won by* walking in obedience *to the only Coach who never loses a game."*

Obedient Worship Still Brings Walls Down

Walls still exist today. Not of stone and mortar, but of injustice, fear, poverty, doubt, depression, and accusation. And while we might want to shout, argue, or fight, God often invites us to walk, to trust, and to obey.

Jericho fell because Joshua didn't rely on his own understanding. He submitted to the strange strategy of heaven. God's ways are higher—and they often look foolish to the world. But in the realm of the Spirit, obedience is louder than noise.

Worship through obedience is not always spectacular. Sometimes, it's walking around the same wall day after day in silence. Sometimes, it's holding your tongue when slander strikes. Sometimes, it's staying faithful in the unseen.

But heaven notices.

When Worship Requires the Process

The Israelites had to obey the full process—seven days of walking. They couldn't skip ahead to the shouting. If they had stopped on day six, they would have forfeited the promise.

Obedient worship means trusting God's timeline, not ours. The breakthrough comes not when we're ready, but when we're aligned with His instruction.

The number seven in the Bible represents completeness. God wasn't just testing their patience—He was perfecting their obedience.

Your Jericho Can Fall Too

Are you facing a Jericho?

Maybe it's a diagnosis. A failing marriage. A prodigal child. A closed door. A wall that will not budge.

Friend, God might be inviting you not to fight, but to walk.

Not to protest, but to praise. Not to prove your strength, but to show your trust.

Obedient worship is not passive—it's powerful. When we follow God's voice instead of our instincts, we tap into a higher realm of warfare. We shift from human striving to divine strategy.

And when heaven sees obedience rooted in worship, walls fall.

So march again. Worship again. Obey again.

Your Jericho will not stand forever.

Chapter 7: David – The Worshipping Warrior King

In the pages of Scripture, no figure embodies the fusion of worship and warfare more completely than David. Shepherd. Psalmist. Giant-slayer. King. His life was a symphony of praise, pain, passion, and purpose. Yet what stands out most in David's journey is not his throne, nor his triumphs—it is his heart of worship.

He was not chosen because of appearance, strength, or social standing. He was chosen because of the posture of his heart—a heart shaped in secret places, tuned to the rhythms of heaven. David's worship was not a performance—it was a life poured out before God in both private intimacy and public reverence.

Worship in the Pasture: Where Kings Are Formed

Before David ever wore a crown, he held a harp.

Long before he was known in Israel, he was known in heaven. His audience was not a crowd, but sheep—and God. Alone in the fields, while tending his father's flock, David cultivated a heart of worship. It was in the pasture that he learned to sing, to play, to listen, and to speak with the Lord. His songs weren't composed for records; they were the cries of a soul in love with his Creator.

"The Lord is my Shepherd; I shall not want." (Psalm 23:1)

"When I consider Your heavens, the work of Your fingers... what is man that You are mindful of him?" (Psalm 8:3–4)

These words weren't written from the throne—they were born in obscurity.

Worship began not with a platform, but with presence. And in that quiet communion, David grew—not just in musical skill, but in spiritual stature. The pasture is where God trains worshippers to become warriors.

Worship in the Palace: The Song that Never Stopped

When Saul's inner torment became unbearable, his servants sought someone who could soothe his spirit.

"One of the servants answered, 'I have seen a son of Jesse of Bethlehem who knows how to play the lyre. He is a brave man and a warrior... and the Lord is with him.'" (1 Samuel 16:18)

Even before he became king, David's worship made room for him in royal courts. His music didn't just entertain—it healed. It calmed. It shifted atmospheres. Saul's demonic torment would ease whenever David played his harp, revealing a profound spiritual law: worship changes the environment.

David didn't play to show off—he played to invite God's presence. And where God dwells, chaos flees.

Yet as David rose in rank and reputation, worship remained his foundation. He danced before the Ark of the Covenant when it returned to Jerusalem (2 Samuel 6:14), even when others—like his wife Michal—mocked him. His worship wasn't bound by dignity or protocol; it was extravagant, honest, and undignified before men but glorious before God.

David's life shows us that public worship is only as powerful as the private worship that fuels it.

Psalms: The Personal Worship Diary of a King

The Book of Psalms is not a liturgical document—it is a diary. A divine journal of a man who laid bare his soul before God in every circumstance.

From triumph to tragedy, from betrayal to repentance, from fear to faith, David sang it all.

"Create in me a clean heart, O God, and renew a right spirit within me." (Psalm 51:10)

"Why, my soul, are you downcast? Why so disturbed within me? Put your hope in God..." (Psalm 42:11)

His psalms were not always polished. They were raw. Real. Honest. They teach us that worship isn't about always having the right words—it's about bringing the real you before the real God.

David didn't compartmentalize his emotions. He sang through his sorrow, cried through his victories, and danced through his pain. Every emotion became an opportunity to worship.

In a world where worship is often confined to stages and scheduled moments, David reminds us that worship is a lifestyle, not an event.

From Shepherd to King: Worship as the Pathway

David's path to the throne wasn't straight. He was anointed as a teenager, but spent years running from Saul, hiding in caves, and facing betrayal from those closest to him. Yet, he never lost his worship.

It sustained him when the promise seemed delayed.

In 1 Samuel 30, when David returned to Ziklag and found it burned, his wives and children taken, and his own men threatening to stone him, Scripture says:
"But David encouraged himself in the Lord his God." (1 Samuel 30:6)
When everyone turned, David turned to worship. He remembered who God was. And from that place of renewal, he led again.
Worship wasn't a reaction—it was his foundation.

A Modern Reflection: Jonah Myers – Worship in the Waiting
Jonah Myers was a 28-year-old worship leader from Cape Town, South Africa. He'd spent years recording music, serving in church, and praying for revival. When a major international label discovered his music online, they signed him for an album.
The dream was finally coming true. Until, just days before the album release, a personal health crisis hit—leukemia. Tours canceled. Plans paused. Hospital rooms replaced concert halls.
At first, Jonah spiraled. Confused. Angry. Silent.
But slowly, he began singing again—this time not in studios, but in sterile hospital corridors. Nurses would find him humming psalms at dawn. Patients began requesting worship sessions in the cancer ward.
Jonah's songs, now filled with deeper oil, reached farther than before. Not just notes—but healing. One night, with IV lines still in place, he recorded a raw acoustic version of Psalm 91 on his phone. That single video went viral, touching millions worldwide.
Years later, fully recovered, Jonah now tours with a message not of fame, but of faithfulness.
"I used to lead worship," he told an audience in Johannesburg. *"Now I live worship."*

The Warrior King Still Teaches Us

David's story isn't just history—it's invitation. You may not be a shepherd or a king, but you are called to be a worshipper.

Worship is not merely about music. It is about movement—from pain to praise, from the pasture to the palace, from anonymity to purpose.

Your worship has the power to shift things. To heal. To elevate. To fight. To restore.

David didn't become king because he sought the throne—he became king because he sought the heart of God.

"I have found David son of Jesse, a man after My own heart; he will do everything I want him to do." (Acts 13:22)

May you, like David, worship in the cave and in the court. May your life sing when others are silent. And may your story echo this truth:

Those who live in worship will rise in victory.

Chapter 8:
Jesus – The Ultimate Worshipper

When we speak of worship, our minds often turn to music, singing, or sacred spaces. But the life of Jesus shows us that the truest worship is not in the melody of our lips, but in the surrender of our will. In every step He took, every word He spoke, every act He performed—Jesus worshipped the Father. His entire life was a love song of obedience, a symphony of submission, and a sacrifice of praise.

He is not just the One we worship. He is the worshipper we are called to imitate.

The Gospels record moments when Jesus sang, but they overwhelmingly emphasize His posture of reverence, surrender, and trust, even when walking toward pain. His worship wasn't confined to the synagogue or the temple—it was embodied in every moment, even in the shadow of the Cross.

The Hymn Before the Agony

In Matthew 26:30, a seemingly small detail hides profound meaning:

"And when they had sung a hymn, they went out to the Mount of Olives."

This moment comes just after the Last Supper and just before Jesus enters Gethsemane, where His soul would be overwhelmed with sorrow. Sandwiched between fellowship and suffering, we find worship.

Jesus sang.

What did He sing? Most likely, the Hallel Psalms (Psalms 113–118)—a traditional part of the Passover celebration. These psalms include lines like:

"The Lord is my strength and my defense; He has become my salvation." (Psalm 118:14)
"Precious in the sight of the Lord is the death of His faithful servants." (Psalm 116:15)

He sang of deliverance, knowing He was about to be delivered to death. He sang of God's unfailing love, even as betrayal was unfolding. He sang of victory, knowing the road ahead led through a tomb.

This is worship in its purest form: a declaration of God's faithfulness when the future feels uncertain. For Jesus, worship wasn't a coping mechanism—it was a compass. It pointed Him toward the Father, not away from the pain.

Total Surrender: The Highest Form of Worship

In Gethsemane, we see worship not with strings and songbooks, but with sweat and sorrow.

"And going a little farther, He fell on His face and prayed, saying, 'My Father, if it is possible, let this cup pass from Me. Nevertheless, not as I will, but as You will.'" (Matthew 26:39)

This is the crescendo of Christ's worship.

He wasn't singing here. He was submitting. And that submission was louder in heaven than any choir.

Jesus shows us that worship isn't always pleasant. Sometimes it sounds like weeping. Sometimes it looks like wrestling. Sometimes it feels like laying down your right to be understood, vindicated, or delivered. But the moment of surrender is the moment worship becomes fire on the altar.

When Jesus said, *"Not My will, but Yours,"* He wasn't defeated—He was enthroning God's will above His own pain. That is worship.

Victories Through Submission and Communion

What followed in the next hours was brutal. Betrayal. Beatings. Mockery. A crown of thorns. Nails through flesh. Darkness.

Yet, through every moment of the Passion, Jesus was still worshipping. Not in silence, but in communion.

"Father, forgive them…" (Luke 23:34)

"My God, My God, why have You forsaken Me?" (Matthew 27:46)

"Into Your hands I commit My spirit." (Luke 23:46)

These weren't just final words. They were echoes of Psalms, deep cries of a soul tethered to the Father even in abandonment. Jesus' victory was not only won on the Cross—it was revealed there. The victory had already been sealed in Gethsemane, in that sacred place of surrender.

The Resurrection three days later was not just a reversal of death—it was the reward of worship. It declared once and for all that surrender to the Father never leads to defeat—it leads to glory.

A Contemporary Reflection: Sarah Devlin – Worshiping through the Fire

Sarah Devlin, a schoolteacher in rural England, had never known tragedy. At 33, she was a newlywed, devoted to her small community church, and known for leading gentle hymns every Sunday. Worship for her had always been sweet—a balm, a blessing.

Until her husband Daniel was diagnosed with an aggressive neurological condition six months into their marriage.

As his body declined rapidly, Sarah's songs changed. They weren't loud or triumphant anymore. But they were deeper. One night, after returning from a grueling hospital visit, she sat at her piano and whispered, *"Though You slay me, yet will I trust You."* That night, she wrote a simple song, born from pain and love, and posted it online.

What happened next surprised her. Thousands of people shared the song. It reached people walking through their own valleys—widows, caregivers, people with terminal diagnoses.

A year later, after Daniel passed away in her arms, Sarah said something during a small house gathering:

"I thought worship was about feeling joy. But now I know it's about faithfulness, *even when you feel forsaken. Jesus taught me that."*

Sarah's worship, like Jesus', became the fragrance of surrender, rising higher than the ashes of her grief. She now leads retreats for women walking through loss, helping them rediscover the God who weeps—and who wins.

Follow the Worshipper Who Wore Thorns

Jesus never asked us to worship Him in a way He wasn't willing to model. He lived it. He walked it. He bled it. From Bethlehem's cradle to Calvary's Cross, His life was an unbroken melody of obedience, love, and reverence.

We often think of victory as strength and conquest. But in the Kingdom of God, the highest victory was achieved through a bowed head, a broken body, and a surrendered will.

The next time you lift your hands in worship, remember His nail-scarred hands. When you lift your voice, remember His cry on the Cross. And when you walk through your own Gethsemane, remember: you are never closer to heaven than when you say, “Not my will, but Yours.”

Worship isn’t only about the songs we sing. It’s about the lives we lay down.

“Have this mind among yourselves, which is yours in Christ Jesus… He humbled Himself by becoming obedient to the point of death—even death on a cross.” (Philippians 2:5, 8)

And because of that obedience, God highly exalted Him**.**

There is no greater worshipper than Jesus.

And no greater invitation than to follow Him in the song of surrender.

PART III:
VICTORIOUS WORSHIP TODAY – REAL LIFE EXAMPLES

Chapter 9: Worship in Modern Warfare – Real Stories

Worship is not a relic of ancient times. It is not confined to the dusty pages of Scripture or the echo of psalms sung in candlelit sanctuaries. Worship remains the weapon of choice for believers across the world facing spiritual, emotional, and even physical battles. Today, just as in biblical times, praise still confounds enemies, faith still moves mountains, and worship still opens prison doors.

In a world filled with wars—both visible and invisible—worship is the battle strategy of heaven.

In this chapter, we explore three modern-day victories won through the power of worship. Though each setting is different—a jungle village, a persecuted city, and a quiet chapel—they share a common theme: when God's people worship, He shows up.

The Emmanuel Family – Worship in the Shadow of Death

The Emmanuel family—Stephen, Ruth, and their two young children, Caleb and Zoe—were missionaries in a dense region of Southeast Asia. They lived in a remote jungle village where tribal warfare and spiritual animism often collided with violent force. Their mission was simple: bring the Gospel to the unreached, live among the people, and show the love of Jesus.

One rainy evening, word spread through the village that a radical militant group, opposed to Western presence and Christian influence, was planning to raid and burn their home. The group had already destroyed two mission outposts nearby, and their threats were never empty.

As fear crept into the hearts of their neighbors, the Emmanuels gathered in their small hut, lit a single oil lamp, and began to sing.

They sang *"Great Is Thy Faithfulness,"* and then moved into a chorus Ruth had written in her quiet time weeks earlier:

"You are the fire in the dark, You are the shield through the storm, I will not fear the night— Your praise will be my war cry."

They sang until midnight. Their children sang with them—shaky voices clinging to a steady God. The family had no weapons, no escape route, no protection—only worship.

At dawn, the village elder came running to their hut. *"The raiders turned back,"* he gasped. "*They stopped a mile from here. No one understands why."*

Later, a local convert explained what the rebels had said: *"We saw fire circling your home, and we heard voices—many voices—singing. We thought you had an army."*

Stephen and Ruth wept. They had no army—only praise. But heaven responded to their worship with divine defense. Like Jehoshaphat centuries before, they learned that sometimes you don't have to fight when you choose to praise.

The Church in Ashra – Worship That Endured the Flames

In a city tucked between the mountains of a politically volatile region in North Africa, stood a small underground church in the district of Ashra. For years, this church gathered in basements, abandoned buildings, and homes behind shuttered windows. Their songs were whispered, their prayers soft, their gatherings illegal.

But they worshipped nonetheless.

One Sunday, during a secret night service, thirty believers gathered in a warehouse to sing. They knew the risks. Police surveillance had increased. Neighbors had been questioned. But they couldn't stop gathering. That night, the worship leader, Miriam, led with a trembling voice as she opened Psalm 27:

"The Lord is my light and my salvation—whom shall I fear?"

Before the third song could end, the police raided. Lights burst in. People were dragged away. The building was set on fire as a warning to others. Miriam was among those arrested.

But something unexpected happened. In the detention center, Miriam kept singing.

At first, just a hum. Then a quiet verse of *"Be Thou My Vision."* Other inmates—Muslims, agnostics, political prisoners—started listening. Days passed. Her jail cell became a chapel. Guards started pausing to listen. One of them, Kareem, who had been harsh at first, returned night after night to hear her sing.

Months later, after her release, Kareem found her again. This time, not to arrest her, but to thank her. *"Your songs wouldn't leave my head,"* he said. *"I heard them in my dreams. I saw the peace in your face. I want to know this Jesus."*

Miriam smiled. The building had burned, but the church had grown. Through whispered worship, God had ignited revival. Persecution had produced praise—and praise had produced salvation.

Daniel Ramesh – Healing at the Altar of Worship

Daniel Ramesh was not just a worship leader—he was a prodigy. At twenty-nine, he had led worship at global conferences, produced three albums, and mentored dozens of younger musicians. But behind the stage lights and songwriting sessions, Daniel had been quietly battling a rare autoimmune disease that slowly drained his energy, caused nerve pain, and left him unable to lift his guitar for long periods.

Doctors had warned him: *"You might need to stop all physical exertion—including playing instruments—within a year."*

The news was devastating. Daniel went silent. He canceled tours. He stopped composing. He didn't blame God, but his heart was numb.

Then one Sunday, his pastor asked him to attend a worship night—not to lead, just to sit and soak.

During the second song, an old hymn was played: *"I Surrender All."* Daniel didn't plan to sing. But when the congregation reached the chorus, he found himself standing, arms raised—pain shooting through his shoulders—tears streaming down his face.

"All to Thee, my blessed Savior, I surrender all…"

He fell to his knees and began to worship with groanings too deep for words.

That night, something shifted. He felt warmth rush through his arms. He could suddenly move without pain. He didn't say anything at first—afraid to believe it. But a week passed. Then a month. He was completely pain-free.

When he returned to the doctor, the scans were clear. *"It's like your immune system reset,"* the specialist said. *"This doesn't make sense."*

But Daniel knew it did. His healing had come not through therapy or treatment—but through total surrender in worship.

Today, Daniel travels again—not as a performer, but as a wounded healer. He shares his testimony, leads people into moments of raw surrender, and tells them:

"Worship doesn't always change your circumstances. But sometimes, it changes your body. Your soul. Your future."

Worship Is Still Winning Battles

In different corners of the world—from jungles and prison cells to urban churches and quiet chapels—worship is still making headlines in heaven. It silences fear, disarms enemies, opens prison doors, heals the body, and births revival.

These are not fairy tales. These are modern altars, built with tears and praise. Just like in Jericho, Gethsemane, and Philippi, God still responds when His people worship—not because we earn a response, but because He inhabits the praises of His people (Psalm 22:3).

So wherever you are, and whatever battle you're facing, remember: your worship matters. It is not weak. It is not invisible. It is not lost.

It is warfare.

And God is still fighting for those who worship.

Chapter 10: When Worship Seems Silent – Still Victorious

Worship is often imagined as music, dancing, clapping, or lifting hands in joyful celebration. But what happens when the music fades? When the voice cracks under the weight of grief? When the heart is too shattered to sing, and silence replaces the sound?

Is that still worship?

The answer from both Scripture and life is a resounding yes.

Some of the most powerful worship ever recorded rose not from the mountaintops, but from the valleys. It came from ashes, from aching hearts, and from faith that refused to quit even when all external evidence said God had gone silent.

This chapter explores the quiet, almost invisible, yet deeply potent worship of endurance—a worship that says, *"Even if He does not..."* (Daniel 3:18). It is the worship of loss, of waiting, and of weeping—and it is just as victorious as the shout of praise.

Horatio Spafford – Worship in the Ashes

Horatio Spafford's story is etched into Christian memory through the timeless hymn *"It Is Well With My Soul."* But few grasp the depth of darkness from which that hymn was birthed.

A wealthy Chicago lawyer in the 19th century, Spafford was a man of deep faith. In 1871, the Great Chicago Fire ravaged his investments and real estate holdings. Two years later, as part of a planned trip to

Europe for rest and ministry, he sent his wife and four daughters ahead by ship, planning to follow soon after.

Midway across the Atlantic, their vessel collided with another and sank. All four daughters perished. Only his wife, Anna, survived. When Spafford received her telegram—*"Saved alone…"*—he boarded the next ship to meet her. As his ship passed over the location where his daughters had drowned, he stood on the deck, silent.

Then, quietly, words formed in his heart:

"When peace like a river attendeth my way,
When sorrows like sea billows roll;
Whatever my lot, Thou hast taught me to say,
It is well, it is well with my soul."

He didn't shout. He didn't sing aloud. But in that still, sacred moment of surrender, he worshipped.

Spafford's life reminds us that worship is not always loud. Sometimes, it's silent submission, a whisper in the storm, a tear-streaked declaration that God is still good, even when life is not.

Rina's Story – Worship in the Waiting Room

Rina D'Costa was a quiet, middle-aged woman living in Hyderabad. She worked as a school secretary, faithfully attended her small church, and lived alone after losing her parents early in life. But what made Rina's story unique wasn't her outward life—it was the interior war she waged for decades.

At 28, she had been diagnosed with a rare hormonal disorder that made pregnancy unlikely. Though she deeply desired marriage and motherhood, suitors came and went—some offended by her honesty, others dismissing her faith.

By her mid-40s, many assumed she had simply settled into singlehood.

But they didn't see the hours she spent at her small altar each morning, Bible open, sometimes saying nothing at all—just waiting. Waiting with hope, waiting in pain, waiting in worship.

Rina often said, "Waiting is not wasted when it's done in His presence." She had no songs, no platforms, and no miracles to show the world. But her life was a living psalm, penned slowly with each sunrise she met in surrender.

At 49, Rina adopted a baby girl who had been abandoned at a railway station. *"God didn't forget me," she told her church softly. "He just answered differently."*

Her worship didn't bring what she wanted when she wanted—but it brought peace, purpose, and presence. And that was enough.

Zach and Amara – Worship Amidst the Rubble

Zach and Amara Owusu were a young Ghanaian couple serving as relief workers in Turkey during the 2023 earthquake crisis. On the final day of their humanitarian mission, the unthinkable happened—a second tremor struck the area. In the chaos, their son Eli, just six years old, was separated from them. Despite days of searching, his body was found under the rubble.

The grief was paralyzing. Amara, a worship leader, stopped singing. Zach resigned from preaching. Friends rallied, but the silence in their home was deafening.

Weeks passed.

One evening, Amara sat alone in the guest room where her son had last slept. She found his Bible on

the shelf, the one he had scribbled in during family devotions. On the front page, in uneven handwriting, were the words: *"Jesus is with me. I love Him back."*
That night, she did not sing. But she knelt. She raised her hands. And in between sobs, she whispered: *"Jesus, I still love You back."*
It was not a song. It was not a sermon. But it was worship—pure and unfiltered. A surrender soaked in sorrow, yet filled with love.
Weeks later, Amara returned to church. The first song she led was *"Way Maker."* She couldn't finish the chorus. The congregation sang it for her—on her behalf.
And heaven received every note.

Biblical Echoes – Job, Hannah, and Jesus
Scripture is rich with those who worshipped in silence, loss, and waiting.
Job, after losing everything—his children, his wealth, his health—fell to the ground and worshipped (Job 1:20). He didn't understand. He received no explanations. But he worshipped because he knew God was still worthy, even when life was not fair.
Hannah, tormented by barrenness, poured out her soul before the Lord—not with eloquence, but with tears (1 Samuel 1). Her lips moved. No sound was heard. But her silent anguish became an offering, and God answered her heart's cry.
And Jesus—oh, the quiet worship of Gethsemane. The Son of God, bowed under the weight of sin and sorrow, sweating blood, saying, *"Not my will, but Yours be done."* No song. No harp. But in that moment, ***the highest act of worship ever known***—total surrender—was given.

When the Song Ceases, Worship Remains

Worship doesn't end when the music does. In fact, some of the greatest victories in the Kingdom are won in the silence between songs.

When you've prayed and nothing changed.

When you've waited and no answer came.

When you've wept and still said, "Yet will I praise You."

That is victorious worship.

Worship in silence is not the absence of faith. It is the deepest kind of faith—the faith that believes even when there is no sound, no sign, no sensation.

And God hears it all.

He hears the silence.

He receives the tears.

He crowns the endurance.

So when worship seems silent—when you feel like there's nothing left to offer—remember, your very breath is worship, your waiting is worship, and your refusal to let go of God is the anthem that echoes in heaven.

And that kind of worship—though quiet—is never wasted.

It is always victorious.

PART IV:
BECOMING A TRUE WORSHIPPER – A PRACTICAL TRANSFORMATIONAL GUIDE

Chapter 11:
The Worshipper's Identity

The journey of becoming a true worshipper doesn't begin with music, talent, or stage presence—it begins with identity.

Until we understand *who we are*, we will always strive to *perform* rather than *worship*. Worship is not something we do to impress God or others; it is an outflow of who we are as His redeemed sons and daughters—priests, kings, and beloved children created for His glory.

In a world that idolizes talent and visibility, reclaiming our identity as true worshippers is one of the most countercultural and necessary shifts for every believer. This chapter explores what it means to walk in that identity with depth, purpose, and power.

You Are a Royal Priesthood

When the Apostle Peter declared, *"But you are a chosen generation, a royal priesthood, a holy nation, His own special people…"* (1 Peter 2:9), he wasn't merely offering poetic encouragement. He was restoring purpose and dignity to every believer.

In the Old Testament, priests were exclusively selected from the tribe of Levi. Their role was to minister before the Lord, offer sacrifices, and intercede for the people. Kings, on the other hand, ruled with authority. The two roles were distinct and rarely overlapped.

But in Christ, we are made both.

We carry the intimacy of the priest and the authority of the king. Worship is where both of those identities meet. In worship, we minister to the heart of God as priests, and we release heaven's decree on earth as kings. We stand before the throne not as beggars or entertainers—but as those called, cleansed, and commissioned.

Created to Worship

Revelation 4:11 declares, *"You are worthy, O Lord, to receive glory and honor and power; for You created all things, and by Your will they exist and were created."*

Worship is not optional. It is the very reason we exist. God didn't create humanity to entertain Him or to labor for Him. He created us for fellowship, for communion, for worship. Worship is not merely a spiritual activity—it is the essence of our being.

Every human being, whether knowingly or not, is a worshipper. The only question is who or what are we worshipping? Some worship money. Others worship fame, security, or even themselves. But only in worship directed toward God do we discover our true fulfillment and eternal purpose.

Worship is not limited to a Sunday service. It is the posture of our entire life—how we love, give, forgive, serve, and live in obedience.

Worshippers vs Performers

One of the great tragedies in modern Christianity is the confusion between worship and performance.

A performer seeks applause. A worshipper seeks His presence.

A performer worries about sound and style. A worshipper is consumed by surrender and substance.

A performer draws eyes to themselves. A worshipper points all eyes to Jesus.

This confusion isn't limited to music ministries. It seeps into pulpits, platforms, and even personal devotion. We can turn our quiet times into boxes to check off, our prayers into public displays, our service into something to be praised for—instead of poured out as worship.

The Story of Elias Mathews – The Performer Who Forgot to Worship

Elias Mathews was a gifted pianist and worship leader in a large church in South Africa. By all appearances, he had it all—musical genius, a loyal following, and weekly standing ovations from the congregation.

But inwardly, Elias was empty.

He confessed later, "*I was performing for people, not ministering to God.*" He would practice hours to perfect every chord but spend mere minutes in prayer. He relied on applause to feel validated, not the presence of the Holy Spirit. Worship had become a stage, not an altar.

Then one evening, during a conference, the power failed. The lights went out. The sound system shut down. Chaos broke out in the auditorium.

Elias stood silently behind the keyboard.

And then he began to play—without electricity, without spotlight, without anyone watching.

A single, spontaneous melody. No lyrics. Just tears.

And in that moment, he found God again.

That was the last night Elias led worship from a stage. He stepped down from the worship team, not out of shame, but out of reverence. *"I needed to remember who I am—a son, not a performer,"* he said.

Elias now leads worship in small prayer gatherings, in orphanages, and on the street corners of

Johannesburg. The crowds are smaller—but the glory is deeper.

A Worshipping Identity Transforms Everything

When you know you are a worshipper by design, it shifts your entire life:

- ✓ Work becomes worship when done with excellence unto the Lord.
- ✓ Relationships become worship when love flows sacrificially.
- ✓ Suffering becomes worship when it is endured with trust.
- ✓ Obedience becomes worship when done out of reverence, not duty.

Mariah's Quiet Worship – The Stay-at-Home Intercessor

Mariah Jacob was not a singer. She was not a preacher. She was a 67-year-old widow living in a small village near Kochi. Her life seemed invisible to the outside world.

But in heaven's eyes, she was known.

Every morning at 5 a.m., she lit a candle, opened her worn Bible, and began to worship. No music. No microphone. Just faith. She would pray for families, pastors, children, missionaries, and strangers.

She would sing softly, out of tune, yet fully in love.

People in her village often called her *"the candle lady"* because the window of her house always glowed before dawn. What they didn't realize was that her home had become a tabernacle, and her worship was changing the atmosphere.

Years later, when her funeral was held, dozens testified that their breakthroughs, healing, and protection had come because *"Amma Mariah prayed."*

Her identity wasn't in titles. It was in worship. And it transformed everything she touched.

Jesus: The Perfect Picture of Identity in Worship
Jesus, the ultimate worshipper, operated fully in His identity. At His baptism, before He had preached a sermon or performed a miracle, the Father said, *"This is My beloved Son, in whom I am well pleased."* (Matthew 3:17).

Jesus did not minister for *identity. He ministered* from *identity.*

This is the foundation of true worship.

Worship that flows from a secure identity is not shaken by applause or rejection. It is not shaped by performance, but by presence.

Embracing Who You Really Are
You are not just a worker in God's kingdom.

You are not just a church attendee or a voice in the choir.

You are not what you do.

You are a worshipper.

Chosen. Royal. Holy. Beloved.

The moment you stop striving to *be seen* and start living to *see Him*, your worship becomes real. It becomes powerful. It becomes transformational.

Lay down the act. Leave behind the performance. Come boldly to the throne, not as an artist—but as a priest and king.

That is who you are.

That is the identity of a true worshipper

Chapter 12: The Worshipper's Heart – Character Over Charisma

In today's performance-driven culture, charisma is often mistaken for anointing. Talent draws crowds, but character draws God. God does not delight in flawless melodies if the heart is far from Him. This is why the heart of a worshipper matters more than the gift they bring.

The Condition of the Heart is the True Instrument
"People look at the outward appearance, but the Lord looks at the heart." (1 Samuel 16:7)
King David was a skilled harpist, but that was not what qualified him. He was *"a man after God's own heart"* (Acts 13:22). His psalms were not polished performances—they were raw prayers, often written in caves and conflict.
Contrast this with King Saul, who started with favor and public approval but lost his position because of disobedience. Saul offered a burnt offering out of fear, stepping into the priest's role, not because of love or reverence—but out of impatience and pride (1 Samuel 13). His worship was compromised. His heart was not aligned with God's will.
Worship that God Rejects
In Isaiah 29:13, the Lord laments, *"These people come near to me with their mouth and honor me with their lips, but their hearts are far from me."* This verse is a sobering reminder that worship without sincerity is offensive to God.

Mikhail Joshi, a fictional worship leader in Chennai, had a booming ministry and was often invited to large events. But behind closed doors, he struggled with pride, manipulation, and bitterness toward fellow musicians. One night, after leading thousands in worship, he felt an emptiness he couldn't explain.

Later that week, during a small group, a woman timidly sang a simple worship song off-key, but with tears streaming down her face. Mikhail said, "For the first time in years, I felt the Lord's presence in a song not my own." That night, he fell on his knees and repented. He stepped back from ministry for a year to rebuild not his platform—but his heart.

Worship isn't measured in decibels or stage presence. It's measured in obedience, purity, and humility. It's about character over charisma.

The Worshipper's Hidden Life

God honors the unseen life. Worship happens when no one is watching—when you forgive quietly, serve joyfully, give generously, and repent sincerely.

Naomi Griggs, a fictitious grandmother from Kentucky, worshipped God faithfully in her living room every morning with a cup of coffee and her old Bible. She had no platform, no title, no microphone. But her children and grandchildren watched her love the Lord for decades. Her prayers helped birth three pastors and one missionary. Her worship shaped generations.

Worshippers like Naomi may not trend on social media, but Heaven knows their voice.

Chapter 13: Barriers to Worship – What Holds Us Back

If worship is the most intimate expression of our relationship with God, then it is no surprise that the enemy works relentlessly to hinder it. Worship not only glorifies God—it transforms us. It softens our hearts, realigns our priorities, and welcomes the very presence of heaven into our lives. This is why barriers to worship are not just inconveniences—they are battlegrounds.

Many believers struggle with worship not because they lack desire, but because something holds them back. These barriers can be internal or external, subtle or obvious. They often creep into our lives unnoticed until our heart feels dry, our songs feel empty, and our connection with God seems distant.

This chapter explores those barriers—pride, performance, fear, pain, distraction, religion, guilt, shame, and apathy—and how the Lord graciously leads us through them into deeper intimacy.

The Silent Wall of Pride

Pride is perhaps the most deceptive and dangerous barrier to worship. It whispers that we are self-sufficient, too important, or too composed to bow, weep, or lift our hands in surrender.

In the story of the Pharisee and the tax collector (Luke 18:10–14), Jesus draws a sharp contrast. The Pharisee stands tall, listing his accomplishments. He fasts, gives, and avoids sin. But his heart is closed.

The tax collector, broken and humble, can barely lift his eyes. He beats his chest and cries for mercy.
Jesus says the tax collector, not the Pharisee, went home justified.
Worship begins with humility. Pride cannot coexist with true adoration. It resists the vulnerability worship requires.

Jonathan Samuel – The CEO in the Front Row

Jonathan Samuel was a prominent CEO in Mumbai. A dignified man of poise, intelligence, and accomplishment. Though he had attended church for years, he had never once raised his hands in worship. *"It's not my personality,"* he would say.
But it wasn't personality. It was pride.
One Sunday, during a worship session, a young girl sang softly, *"I surrender all…"* Her voice was simple, untrained—but pure. Something broke inside Jonathan. Tears welled up in his eyes as he realized that he had never truly surrendered anything—not his time, his pride, or his identity.
He whispered to God, *"I don't want to hold back anymore."*
That day, he knelt on the polished marble floor in his designer suit, hands lifted, tears flowing. Pride had been his wall—but worship broke it.

The Trap of Performance

When worship becomes a task to complete or a show to execute, we lose its essence.
Performance-driven worship says: *"Am I good enough? Did I hit the right note? Did people respond?"* But true worship says: *"Was God glorified? Was my heart offered fully?"*
This struggle is evident in Martha, the sister of Mary (Luke 10:38–42). While Martha is busy serving—

doing good things—Mary sits at Jesus' feet in adoration. Jesus does not rebuke Martha's work but points out that Mary chose the better part.

Worship is not measured by productivity, but by presence.

Rina Thomas – The Perfectionist Worship Leader

Rina led worship every Sunday at her local church in Kerala. She rehearsed tirelessly, arranged harmonies, and fine-tuned every transition. But her soul was dry. The congregation sang, but heaven felt silent.

One morning, during a personal devotion, she read Psalm 51:17: *"The sacrifices of God are a broken spirit; a broken and contrite heart, these, O God, You will not despise."*

That morning, she left her guitar behind. She simply sat before God and cried. No music. No microphone. Just surrender. That became the turning point. From that day on, she stopped performing. She started ministering—to the Lord, and then to people.

Fear, Pain, and Distraction – The Subtle Saboteurs

Fear holds us back—fear of judgment, failure, vulnerability. Pain hardens our hearts. Distraction scatters our attention.

Even King David—mighty worshipper and psalmist—knew moments of anguish. In Psalm 13, he cries, *"How long, O Lord? Will You forget me forever?"* But even in his questioning, David returns to worship: *"But I have trusted in Your mercy; my heart shall rejoice in Your salvation."*

Anjali Das – The Silent Worshipper

Anjali was a new believer, recently rescued from an abusive relationship. She found Jesus in a small house church in rural Bihar. Every time the music started, she froze. She couldn't sing. Her trauma was still too raw.

One day, the pastor said, *"Even silence can be worship—if your heart is reaching toward Him."*

From that moment on, Anjali began to worship with tears, eyes closed, arms open. Slowly, her heart healed. Her silence turned into whispers. Whispers turned into song. Pain had once held her captive—but worship set her free.

The Religious Spirit vs. Relationship

The religious spirit emphasizes *form over heart*, *ritual over relationship*, *tradition over transformation*.

Jesus confronted this often. In Mark 7:6–7, He quoted Isaiah, saying, *"These people honor Me with their lips, but their heart is far from Me. And in vain they worship Me…"*

Religion without relationship produces *performance*, *judgment*, and *distance*.

Pastor Daniel Roy – The Rule Keeper

Daniel Roy pastored a conservative church in Tamil Nadu. Everything was orderly—hymns sung precisely, prayers timed perfectly, and worship services strictly structured.

But something was missing.

When his teenage daughter fell severely ill, Daniel found himself unable to recite prayers. In desperation, he began to worship alone, on his knees. No script. No schedule. Just raw, trembling praise.

He said later, *"For years, I led worship with my lips. That night, I worshipped with my life."*

The church changed. Spontaneity emerged. Hearts softened. Joy returned. Religion gave way to relationship.

Guilt, Shame, and Apathy – The Hidden Killers

Guilt whispers, *"You're unworthy."*
Shame shouts, *"You're disqualified."*
Apathy sighs, *"Why bother?"*
But the cross of Christ answers them all.
Romans 8:1 declares, *"There is therefore now no condemnation to those who are in Christ Jesus."*
Hebrews 10:22 says, *"Let us draw near with a true heart in full assurance of faith, having our hearts sprinkled from an evil conscience…"*

Tariq George – The Former Addict

Tariq had a criminal record, a history of drug addiction, and a life full of regret. When he walked into a church in Punjab, heads turned. He didn't belong—at least not by human standards.
But one worship session, as the church sang *"Come Just As You Are,"* he broke. He fell to the floor and wept uncontrollably. A church elder knelt beside him and said, *"God isn't ashamed of you, son. He's been waiting."*
Tariq was never the same. He now leads worship at a rehabilitation center. His voice is rough, his past is dark—but his worship is pure.

The Path to Freedom

God does not condemn us for the barriers we carry. He invites us to bring them to Him.
He breaks pride with love.
He dismantles performance with presence.
He heals fear with security.
He melts pain with compassion.

He pierces distraction with glory.
He replaces religion with intimacy.
He washes guilt and shame with the blood of Jesus.
He revives apathy with His fire.

Worship is not reserved for the perfect. It is the *pathway* for the broken. It is not about ability—it is about availability.

Tear Down the Walls

If something is holding you back from worship, it is not a disqualification—it is an invitation. Bring your fears. Bring your past. Bring your wounds, your questions, your silence.

Jesus, the One who tore the veil, invites you into a place where no barrier remains.

You don't need to perform. You don't need to be strong. You just need to come.

The Father is seeking worshippers—not for their sound, but for their surrender.

Let nothing hold you back.

Chapter 14: The Language of Worship – Word, Song, Silence, and Sacrifice

Worship is not confined to melodies or liturgies. It is the expression of the soul's deepest longing toward the One who made it. Just as human language has many dialects and expressions, so too does worship have its languages—each revealing a different posture of the heart.

Some worship with declarations and proclamations. Some through music and melody. Others bow in stillness and silence. And yet, worship that costs us—worship through sacrifice—often speaks the loudest in heaven.

This chapter explores four powerful expressions of worship: Spoken Word, Song, Silence, and Sacrifice. Each is vital. Each is biblical. Each tells heaven, *"He is worthy."*

Worship Through Spoken Word – Declaration and Exaltation

In the beginning, God created through speech. He said, *"Let there be…"* and there was (Genesis 1). His Word formed the cosmos.

And we, made in His image, have been given the power of speech to glorify, declare, and lift up His name.

When we speak of God's greatness, when we proclaim His truth aloud—whether in prayer, praise, or prophecy—we participate in a divine act. Spoken worship aligns the atmosphere with heaven's reality.

Biblical Example: David's Declarations

King David was not just a warrior and psalmist—he was a declarer of God's goodness. In Psalm 34:1–3, he proclaims, *"I will bless the Lord at all times; His praise shall continually be in my mouth... Oh, magnify the Lord with me, and let us exalt His name together."*

His worship wasn't limited to song—it was loud, clear, and verbal. He knew the power of his tongue to magnify the Lord and shift spiritual climates.

Reuben D'Costa – The Street Evangelist

Reuben was once a shy and withdrawn college student in Goa. After a radical encounter with Jesus during a gospel camp, he found that worship spilled out of his mouth at unexpected moments. On buses, in tea stalls, while walking to class, he began to boldly speak of God's love, faithfulness, and saving power.

At first, his peers mocked him. Some professors threatened disciplinary action. But Reuben was undeterred. *"If I can speak of cricket and cinema,"* he once said, *"why should I stay silent about the One who saved me?"*

Reuben eventually became a street evangelist, known not just for preaching, but for stopping mid-sermon to declare aloud: *"Jesus, You are worthy of every breath on this street!"* His words weren't scripted—they were worship, and they softened even the hardest hearts.

Musical Worship – Personal and Corporate Expression

Music is the most recognized language of worship. Its power lies in how it engages the mind, soul, and body all at once. It unites congregations and stirs

individuals. It transcends language, culture, and even generation.
The Bible overflows with songs—songs of victory, lament, praise, and prophecy. Musical worship opens doors for heaven to invade earth.

Biblical Example: Paul and Silas in Prison

In Acts 16:25, Paul and Silas, imprisoned and chained for their faith, chose to worship. At midnight, they sang hymns. Not only were they heard by the other prisoners—but God responded. An earthquake shook the foundations of the prison, and the doors flung open.
Their song wasn't entertainment—it was warfare, freedom, and faith on display.

Nalini Raj – The Widow with the Violin

Nalini lived in Chennai and had lost her husband in a tragic accident. For months, she was silent. Her grief felt like a cavern. But one day, she picked up her old violin—the one she hadn't touched in years.
She began playing softly in her room. The notes turned into worship. Each stroke of the bow was a cry, a surrender, a declaration of hope.
Eventually, she joined the church worship team. She never spoke much—but when she played, something happened. Hearts melted. Tears flowed. God was glorified.
Her pastor once said, *"Nalini doesn't play music. She worships through it—and heaven listens."*

Silent Worship – Soaking and Stillness

In a world of noise, silence can be a sacred act. True worship doesn't always require words or melody. Sometimes, the deepest worship happens when we are still before God.

Psalm 46:10 says, *"Be still, and know that I am God."* This kind of worship invites us to lay down our striving, to enter into His presence not to speak—but to behold. Silent worship is the surrender of control. It is listening more than speaking. Waiting more than doing.

Biblical Example: Elijah's Encounter at Mount Horeb

In 1 Kings 19:11–13, Elijah experiences God not in the wind, earthquake, or fire—but in a *still small voice*. Silence, it turns out, can carry the greatest revelation.

Asif Mathew – The Software Engineer

Asif worked in Hyderabad's bustling IT sector. Analytical, driven, and precise, he found church worship services too loud and emotionally charged. But his hunger for God led him to explore solitude.

He began spending time in silent retreats, simply sitting before the Lord, meditating on a single verse or sometimes no verse at all—just His presence.

At first, it felt awkward. But slowly, his heart began to burn. One evening, he sensed God say, *"I delight in your stillness."*

Now, Asif leads a small group focused on contemplative worship. No instruments. No preaching. Just soaking. Just being. And the testimonies? Marriages healed. Anxiety broken. Joy restored. All from silence offered as worship.

Sacrificial Worship – Giving, Forgiving, and Surrender

Worship without cost is often worship without weight. Sacrificial worship is not convenient—it is costly. It may involve giving when it hurts, forgiving when it seems unfair, or surrendering when we'd rather hold on.

God responds powerfully to sacrificial worship. It reveals a heart fully yielded.

Biblical Example: The Woman with the Alabaster Jar

In Luke 7:36–38, a woman enters a Pharisee's house, breaks a costly alabaster flask of perfume, and anoints Jesus' feet. The room is offended by her extravagance. But Jesus is moved.

He calls it beautiful. He says she will be remembered.

Her worship was sacrificial. It cost her reputation, wealth, and safety. But it was pure.

Prakash and Sheela – The Couple Who Gave Their Home

Prakash and Sheela were a retired couple from Pune. They had spent their lives building a modest but comfortable home. One night during prayer, they felt God nudge them: *"Give your house for My Kingdom."*

They didn't understand. But they obeyed.

They sold their home, bought a small flat, and used the funds to start a shelter for homeless women and children. Each morning, they would walk into the shelter, lift their hands, and sing, *"All I have is Yours."*

People called it charity. But they knew it was worship.

Sheela once said, *"My voice may never reach a stage, but my surrender sings in heaven."*

Speak, Sing, Sit, and Surrender

Worship has many expressions. Whether spoken, sung, silent, or sacrificial—what matters is the heart behind it.

Some will lift hands. Others will lift hearts. Some will dance. Others will bow. But all are welcome to bring their own language of worship before the Lord.

He is not listening for perfection—He is listening for authenticity.

Whatever language your heart speaks, let it be real. Let it be full. Let it be yours.

And when your worship becomes the truest expression of your love, then whether you shout or sit, sing or serve—you are speaking heaven's language.

PART V:

ACTION PLAN – LIVING AS A VICTORIOUS WORSHIPPER

Chapter 15: Creating Your Personal Worship Strategy

Worship is more than a feeling or a Sunday morning event. It is a lifestyle. Just as an athlete disciplines his body or a scholar organizes his study schedule, a worshipper must intentionally shape their life around the presence of God. Passion alone is not enough. Without rhythm, structure, and sacred space, passion burns out or becomes scattered.

A personal worship strategy isn't rigid religion—it's sacred rhythm. It's the design of a heart that says, *"Lord, I want to meet with You—not once in a while, but constantly, meaningfully, and wholeheartedly."*

In this chapter, we'll explore how to develop a consistent worship life through daily, weekly, and monthly rhythms, how to create physical and spiritual spaces for worship, how to keep a worship journal, and how to set goals that both ground and grow your worship walk.

Daily, Weekly, and Monthly Worship Rhythms

The lives of great men and women of God have always included rhythms—habitual patterns of seeking God. The Bible says in Daniel 6:10 that *"three times a day, Daniel got down on his knees and prayed, giving thanks to his God, just as he had done before."* Even when threatened with death, Daniel did not break his rhythm of worship.

Likewise, the early church "devoted themselves daily to the apostles' teaching and to the breaking of bread and prayer" (Acts 2:42–46). Worship was not confined to the Sabbath—it was a daily rhythm woven into community and personal life.

Radhika Murthy – The Busy Entrepreneur

Radhika ran a successful catering business in Bengaluru. With 70 employees and daily operations starting at 4 a.m., she struggled for time. But after a near-death experience due to a health scare, she committed to making worship her priority.

Each morning, before stepping into her kitchen, she would spend 15 minutes in personal worship—reading a Psalm, listening to a song, and journaling a short prayer. On Sundays, she'd attend a small house church. Once a month, she would take an early morning walk in a botanical garden to reflect and thank God for the month's journey.

It wasn't dramatic. It wasn't flashy. But it was consistent. Her staff began to notice something different. Her peace. Her joy. Her favor. She simply smiled and said, *"Worship is how I breathe now."*

Designing a "Worship Room" in Your Heart and Home

Worship doesn't require a temple built with stone, but the Bible does speak of dedicated spaces for meeting with God. Jesus often retreated to quiet places (Luke 5:16), and the tabernacle of Moses had a Most Holy Place where the glory of God dwelt (Exodus 25:22).

Today, the true worship room is our heart—but creating a physical space can help train the soul to turn its attention Godward.

Joseph and Naomi D'Lima – The Young Married Couple

Joseph and Naomi were newlyweds in Mumbai. They lived in a compact one-bedroom flat, and space was

tight. But they felt the Lord nudge them to create a corner in their home just for worship.
They moved a shelf, placed a small rug, a lamp, their Bibles, and a speaker for music. Every morning, before starting work, they'd sit in that space—sometimes reading Scripture aloud, sometimes simply listening to worship music in silence.
That little corner became their sanctuary. In that space, Naomi once received a word from the Lord that saved their business. Joseph said, *"It's the smallest space in our house—but heaven visits us there."*
Equally important is creating a "worship room" in your heart. A place always open to God, even in the middle of work, traffic, or turmoil. It's the posture that whispers, *"I am always aware of Your presence."*

The Worship Journal – Recording Your Daily God Moments

In Exodus 17:14, God tells Moses, *"Write this for a memorial in the book..."* God values remembrance. When we journal, we don't just record events—we acknowledge God's presence in our story.
A worship journal helps capture God-moments—those small, sacred encounters that might otherwise be forgotten. It becomes a personal altar of remembrance.

Shyam Sundar – The Retired School Principal

Shyam lived alone in Coimbatore after his wife passed away. With his children abroad, he often felt lonely. One day, while reading Psalm 139, he felt overwhelmed by God's nearness. He grabbed an old notebook and began to write: *"Today, I felt seen by the Lord."*

That was the beginning of his worship journal. Every evening after his walk, he would sit, light a lamp, and write what he felt God was saying—or how he had sensed Him during the day.

Sometimes it was a sunset. Other times a quiet thought. And often, it was simply gratitude.

Years later, his granddaughter found the journal. Reading through it brought her to tears. She gave her life to Christ because of it.

Worship journaling may seem small—but it is sacred. Heaven reads over your shoulder when you write to God.

Setting Worship Goals – Spiritual and Practical

A life of worship needs both heart and direction. Goals give our devotion focus and purpose. They are not for legalism but for growth.

Spiritual goals could include memorizing Scriptures, deepening intimacy, learning new songs, or cultivating silence. Practical goals might include blocking specific times, reducing digital distractions, or attending worship retreats.

Biblical Example: Paul's Pursuit of Knowing Christ

Paul writes in Philippians 3:10, *"That I may know Him…"* This was not a vague wish—it was a life goal. Everything he did was aimed at deeper knowledge and communion with Jesus.

Deborah John – The Worship Leader in the Village Church

Deborah was a vibrant worship leader in a small village church in Kerala. Despite having no formal training, her heart burned with desire to grow in worship. She made a plan: each week, she would

learn one new worship song, study one psalm, and lead one family prayer night.
She also set a quarterly goal: to host a worship evening for neighboring villages.
She wrote her goals in a small diary and tracked them with joy—not pressure. Within a year, she had taught her church 30 new songs, seen three families saved, and raised up two new worship leaders.
She would often say, *"Worship isn't a performance—it's a pursuit. And every pursuit needs direction."*

Worship on Purpose

The goal of creating a personal worship strategy is not to add one more obligation to your life. It is to intentionally shape your soul into a vessel that welcomes the King—daily, weekly, monthly, and forever.
Like building a house, this structure gives your spirit a place to dwell with God.
Let your rhythms guide you.
Let your space prepare you.
Let your journal remind you.
Let your goals stretch you.
Because worship is not just something you do. It is someone you become.

Chapter 16:
The 21-Day Worship Transformation Plan

Transformation does not happen in a moment—it happens through intentional encounters over time. The next 21 days are not about performance, but about posture. As you walk through this journey, expect your heart, habits, and perspective to shift. Each day offers a sacred invitation to draw nearer to God, to exchange heaviness for praise, and to root your identity deeper in worship.

Let's begin this holy pilgrimage.

Day 1: God is Worthy

Scripture Focus: *"You are worthy, our Lord and God, to receive glory and honor and power..." – Revelation 4:11*

Worship Action: Play a worship song that magnifies God's majesty (e.g., "Worthy Is the Lamb"). As you listen or sing, focus solely on His worth, not your needs.

Journaling Prompt: Write a list of 10 things that make God worthy of your worship today. Reflect on one of them.

Declaration of Victory: *"Today, I proclaim: My God is worthy, regardless of my circumstances."*

Day 2: Worshipping Through Worry

Scripture Focus: *"Cast all your anxiety on Him because He cares for you." – 1 Peter 5:7*

Worship Action: Write down your top three worries. Pray over them and symbolically place them at the feet of Jesus. Play a song that brings peace.
Journaling Prompt: How has worry affected your worship? What changes when you worship in the middle of fear?
Declaration of Victory: *"Worry bows at the feet of the One who reigns. I choose peace today."*

Day 3: Surrendering the Schedule
Scripture Focus: *"Be still, and know that I am God." – Psalm 46:10*
Worship Action: Cancel one non-essential activity today. Use that time for worship, stillness, and Scripture meditation.
Journaling Prompt: What is something in your schedule that may be crowding out intimacy with God?
Declaration of Victory: *"I surrender time to the Giver of time. My schedule submits to His sovereignty."*

Day 4: Worship Through Tears
Scripture Focus: *"Those who sow in tears shall reap with shouts of joy." – Psalm 126:5*
Worship Action: Let yourself cry in God's presence today. Bring Him your pain without performance.
Journaling Prompt: What unspoken grief have you been carrying? Write a letter to God about it.
Declaration of Victory: *"My tears are seeds, not weakness. They will bring a harvest of worship."*

Day 5: Breaking the Fear of Man
Scripture Focus: *"The fear of man lays a snare, but whoever trusts in the Lord is safe." – Proverbs 29:25*

Worship Action: Dance, lift your hands, or sing aloud—even if you're alone. Let go of self-consciousness.
Journaling Prompt: What would your worship look like if you didn't care who was watching?
Declaration of Victory: *"I worship for an audience of One. Fear will not silence my song."*

Day 6: The Sacrifice of Praise
Scripture Focus: *"Let us continually offer to God a sacrifice of praise..." – Hebrews 13:15*
Worship Action: Worship today even if you don't feel like it. Offer praise as an act of obedience.
Journaling Prompt: When has it been hardest to praise? What did you discover about God through it?
Declaration of Victory: *"Even in the dry place, I will praise. My offering is worship."*

Day 7: Celebrating God's Goodness
Scripture Focus: *"Taste and see that the Lord is good." – Psalm 34:8*
Worship Action: Make a gratitude list. Sing or shout praises for each item.
Journaling Prompt: What act of God's goodness can you celebrate today?
Declaration of Victory: *"My God is good, and I will not forget His benefits!"*

Day 8: Letting Go of the Past
Scripture Focus: *"Forget the former things; do not dwell on the past." – Isaiah 43:18*
Worship Action: Write down past regrets, then destroy the paper. Declare that your past has no hold.

Journaling Prompt: What part of your past has kept you from full freedom in worship?
Declaration of Victory: *"I am not what I was. I worship from a place of redemption."*

Day 9: Worship in the Waiting
Scripture Focus: *"But those who wait on the Lord shall renew their strength…" – Isaiah 40:31*
Worship Action: Play soft instrumental worship music. Sit in stillness before God without asking for anything.
Journaling Prompt: What are you waiting on God for? How can you wait with worship instead of worry?
Declaration of Victory: *"In the waiting, I will worship. I trust His timing."*

Day 10: Worship Through Work
Scripture Focus: *"Whatever you do, do it all for the glory of God." – 1 Corinthians 10:31*
Worship Action: Do one ordinary task (cleaning, writing, working) as an act of worship. Invite God into it.
Journaling Prompt: How can you turn your daily work into daily worship?
Declaration of Victory: *"Even my labor is worship. My hands honor God today."*

Day 11: The Heart of a Worshipper
Scripture Focus: *"Man looks at the outward appearance, but the Lord looks at the heart." – 1 Samuel 16:7*
Worship Action: Examine your heart before worship. Repent if needed. Then worship in spirit and truth.

Journaling Prompt: Is your heart in alignment with your outward worship? Why or why not?
Declaration of Victory: *"My heart is His altar. I worship in authenticity."*

Day 12: Worshipping with Community
Scripture Focus: *"Where two or three gather in my name, there am I with them." – Matthew 18:20*
Worship Action: Call a friend or family member and worship together—through song, prayer, or thanksgiving.
Journaling Prompt: Who in your life strengthens your worship? How can you encourage them today?
Declaration of Victory: *"I was made for worship—and for worship with others."*

Day 13: Worship Through Scripture
Scripture Focus: *"Your word is a lamp to my feet…" – Psalm 119:105*
Worship Action: Choose a psalm and read it aloud as your worship today.
Journaling Prompt: What verse stood out? Why do you think God highlighted it to you?
Declaration of Victory: *"God's Word is worship to my soul and light to my path."*

Day 14: Worship Through Forgiveness
Scripture Focus: *"Forgive as the Lord forgave you." – Colossians 3:13*
Worship Action: Identify someone you need to forgive. Speak forgiveness aloud before God.
Journaling Prompt: How has unforgiveness hindered your intimacy with God?
Declaration of Victory: *"I release forgiveness and receive freedom. My heart is light in worship."*

Day 15: Childlike Worship
Scripture Focus: *"Unless you become like little children…" – Matthew 18:3*
Worship Action: Express joy in worship today—dance, draw, sing loud, or be playful before God.
Journaling Prompt: When did you last worship with childlike freedom?
Declaration of Victory: *"I am my Father's child. I worship without fear or formality."*

Day 16: Healing Through Worship
Scripture Focus: *"He heals the brokenhearted…" – Psalm 147:3*
Worship Action: Focus your worship today on one area where you need healing. Invite God in.
Journaling Prompt: Where are you broken? What do you want God to heal?
Declaration of Victory: *"Worship is my medicine. The Healer is near."*

Day 17: Worship is Warfare
Scripture Focus: *"The battle is not yours, but God's." – 2 Chronicles 20:15*
Worship Action: Declare a song of victory over a current battle in your life.
Journaling Prompt: What spiritual battle are you facing? What is God saying about it?
Declaration of Victory: *"My praise is a weapon. The enemy flees when I worship."*

Day 18: Worship Through Giving
Scripture Focus: *"Honor the Lord with your wealth…" – Proverbs 3:9*

Worship Action: Give today—money, time, help, or encouragement—as an act of worship.
Journaling Prompt: What do you have that you can offer God as worship today?
Declaration of Victory: *"Giving is worship. I hold nothing back from the One who gave all."*

Day 19: Worship in the Mundane
Scripture Focus: *"Do everything in the name of the Lord Jesus." – Colossians 3:17*
Worship Action: Invite God into every simple task today—driving, cooking, working.
Journaling Prompt: What are three daily tasks you can turn into acts of worship?
Declaration of Victory: *"There is no such thing as ordinary when God is in it. I worship in all I do."*

Day 20: Worship Through Obedience
Scripture Focus: *"To obey is better than sacrifice." – 1 Samuel 15:22*
Worship Action: Obey one nudge from the Holy Spirit today—big or small.
Journaling Prompt: What act of obedience is God calling you to today?
Declaration of Victory: *"My obedience is worship. I say 'yes' to God."*

Day 21: Worship is My Identity
Scripture Focus: *"You are a chosen people, royal priests… to declare the praises of Him." – 1 Peter 2:9*
Worship Action: Create a declaration of who you are as a worshipper. Speak it aloud.
Journaling Prompt: How has your understanding of worship changed in the last 21 days?

Declaration of Victory: *"Worship is not just what I do—it is who I am."*

Chapter 17: Building a Lifestyle of Worship in the Family and Community

Worship was never meant to be confined to a church building or a Sunday morning service. From the beginning, God's desire was that His people would carry His presence into every corner of life—home, marketplace, community, and nation. Worship is not a compartment; it is a continuous current. It is the oxygen of the believer and the atmosphere of Heaven brought down to earth.

When worship becomes a family value and a community expression, it creates a culture where God is not just acknowledged occasionally but is enthroned daily. In this chapter, we will explore how families can make worship a lifestyle, how homes can become altars, how believers can minister worship to others, and how corporate worship can lead to societal transformation.

Worship as a Family Value

In Deuteronomy 6:6-7, Moses commanded the Israelites: *"These commandments that I give you today are to be on your hearts. Impress them on your children. Talk about them when you sit at home and when you walk along the road…"* Worship, according to God's design, was to be taught and practiced within the home, not just at the tabernacle or temple.

Consider the fictional family of Samuel and Lydia Abraham, a young Christian couple raising their three children in a busy urban neighborhood in Hyderabad. Early in their marriage, they made a decision that worship would be a cornerstone of their family life—not just through music, but through reverence, thanksgiving, and the daily acknowledgment of God.

Every morning, before the children left for school, the family would gather for 15 minutes. They read a psalm aloud together, sang a simple song, and prayed. It wasn't perfect. Sometimes the toddler cried, the teenager rolled his eyes, and on some days, Samuel was late for work. But over the years, those moments became anchors.

Their middle child, *Elina*, once said during a youth group session, *"I've seen worship not just in the songs my parents sang but in the way my father forgave unfair treatment at work and how my mother served people who could never repay her."*

Worship was more than music—it was a family rhythm, a value that shaped decisions, speech, and service.

How to Lead Worship at Home

Leading worship at home doesn't require musical ability—it requires spiritual intentionality.

In the Old Testament, fathers were the primary spiritual leaders of the household. Job, for instance, offered sacrifices on behalf of his children regularly (Job 1:5), fearing that they might have sinned. His example reveals a heart that interceded in worship for his family's sanctity. In the New Testament, Paul encouraged husbands to *"love their wives as Christ loved the Church"* (Ephesians 5:25), and such sacrificial love is itself an act of worship.

Darren and Grace D'Silva, a retired couple in Goa, began a tradition during the pandemic. Each Sunday evening, their children and grandchildren would gather on a Zoom call. Darren would read a portion from the Psalms, Grace would lead a familiar hymn, and each family member would share one testimony of gratitude.

What started as a coping mechanism during lockdown became a lifestyle. When their grandson Ryan, a college student in Mumbai, faced depression, it was during one of these worship sessions that he wept and asked the family to pray for him. Healing began that day—not because of eloquence but because of an atmosphere of worship.

Homes become sanctuaries when worship is a regular fixture, not an occasional event. Leading worship at home can be as simple as lighting a candle, reading a scripture, and singing a song. It's not about perfection—it's about presence.

Worship as Ministry to Others

Jesus' encounter with the Samaritan woman at the well (John 4) was centered on worship. He told her: *"True worshippers will worship the Father in spirit and truth."* That conversation didn't happen in a temple—it happened in the middle of her brokenness. She left transformed, and immediately became a witness to her community.

Anish Fernandes, a 28-year-old freelance graphic designer, began volunteering at a rehabilitation center for drug addicts. He wasn't a trained counselor, but he carried a guitar. Every Saturday, he led a time of singing, playing soft worship melodies, and sharing stories of hope. He would often say, *"I don't preach—I just play and let God do the work."*

One evening, *Ravi*, a hardened addict who had resisted every group session, quietly walked in during a worship time. Tears streamed down his face as Anish sang *"Amazing Grace."* That night, Ravi surrendered to Christ—not through a sermon, but through worship.

Worship becomes ministry when we carry it into broken spaces. It becomes a balm, a bridge, and a beckoning to the heart of God.

Corporate Worship and Community Transformation

When a community gathers to worship, the spiritual atmosphere changes. We see this in Acts 2:42-47. The early Church devoted themselves to teaching, fellowship, and prayer—and the result was awe, unity, and favor with the people. Worship in the early Church was communal and contagious.

One powerful biblical example of this is found in 2 Chronicles 20, where King Jehoshaphat sent worshippers ahead of his army. As they sang, *"Give thanks to the Lord, for His love endures forever,"* God set ambushes against their enemies. The battle was won not with swords, but with songs.

In a modern-day parallel, Pastor Nehemiah James of *Restoration Gate Fellowship* in Chennai began organizing quarterly community worship nights in a local park. At first, only 30 people showed up. But over time, drug dealers vacated the area, neighborhood violence decreased, and a local tea vendor began testifying that his health had improved *"ever since those people started singing near my cart."*

The local police chief later remarked at a community meeting, *"Whatever you all are doing there, keep doing it. The atmosphere has changed."*

Worship is not passive—it is prophetic. When communities lift up the name of Jesus, chains break, and darkness retreats.

Worship That Spreads

A lifestyle of worship in the family and community is not about turning every moment into a song but turning every breath into a sacred offering. When families worship, they raise generations who know how to seek God. When communities worship, they build cities that reflect Heaven.

Let us remember that our homes can become altars, our neighborhoods can become sanctuaries, and our acts of worship can become seeds of revival. The more we cultivate worship at home and in the streets, the more we mirror the heartbeat of Heaven—a people created to glorify the One who is worthy.

In the words of Psalm 145:4, *"One generation shall praise Your works to another, and shall declare Your mighty acts."* May we be that generation. And may worship never stop with us—but ripple outward like waves across a thirsty land.

Chapter 18: Worship in the Marketplace – Inviting God into the Everyday

Worship is often misunderstood as something confined to church walls, prayer closets, or musical moments. But the God who created us to worship did not intend for it to be boxed into a Sunday schedule. True worship bleeds into every space we occupy—especially the marketplace, where life unfolds, transactions happen, and influence is exercised.

Worship is Not a Location, It's a Lifestyle

In John 4, Jesus tells the Samaritan woman, *"A time is coming and has now come when the true worshipers will worship the Father in the Spirit and in truth. They are the kind of worshipers the Father seeks."* (John 4:23)

Jesus was shifting worship from geography to heart posture—from sacred mountains to sacred hearts. This means worship belongs at work, in classrooms, across boardroom tables, on construction sites, behind cashier counters, and in Zoom meetings.

Jacob Mutombo, a fictitious Congolese architect working in Johannesburg, grasped this truth. Known in his office for his humility and honesty, Jacob prayed over every project before touching his drafting table. When his firm was contracted to design a large commercial plaza, he was offered a substantial bribe to approve illegal permits. Instead of silently declining, Jacob reported the matter, risking his position. When asked why, he responded, "This job

is worship. I design for a God of integrity. I cannot trade that for money."
Jacob's worship didn't involve a guitar—it involved a choice. His everyday decisions became incense before God. His witness changed the office culture and led two colleagues to Christ.

Biblical Grounding: Daniel in Babylon

Daniel worked in the pagan courts of Babylon—arguably one of the most godless marketplaces in history. Yet, he never compartmentalized his faith. *"Daniel distinguished himself... because an excellent spirit was in him."* (Daniel 6:3)

Daniel worshipped by refusing to defile himself with the king's food. He worshipped by praying openly, even when it could cost him his life. And God honored that lifestyle with favor, influence, and miraculous deliverance.

Worship in the marketplace is not about carrying a Bible to work or blasting worship music in the office. It's about walking in integrity, serving with excellence, honoring others, being faithful in little things, and acknowledging God in all your ways (Proverbs 3:5–6).

Rina Elias, a fictional business consultant in Manila, began setting aside the first 15 minutes of every workday just to thank God and dedicate her schedule to Him. She wrote clients' names in her prayer journal. Over time, clients began telling her how peaceful they felt in her presence. They didn't know it was the fruit of worship—but she did.

A Worshipping Professional Transforms Culture

When we live as worshippers in the marketplace:

Work becomes sacred.

Success is redefined by obedience, not income.
Influence increases because integrity builds trust.
Communities are changed from the inside out.

Jesus, a carpenter, spent more time in the marketplace than in the temple. The first disciples were fishermen, tax collectors, and tradesmen. Worship was not their weekly escape—it was their daily walk.

To live as a victorious worshipper means to worship not just in the secret place, but in the marketplace—where battles are fought, testimonies are born, and lives are won for the Kingdom.

PART VI:
THE REWARD OF THE WORSHIPPER

Chapter 19: What Happens When You Worship Consistently

In the quiet corners of life, where few tread and many overlook, the most extraordinary transformations occur—not through toil or strategy alone, but through consistent worship. A worshipper who abides in God's presence day after day, moment after moment, becomes a conduit of Heaven's glory. Their heart becomes God's resting place, and their life, a testimony to what it means to walk in divine favor and supernatural peace. To worship consistently is not merely to sing or bow or kneel; it is to live from a posture of surrender, awareness, and adoration of God. This kind of life cannot remain ordinary—it begins to radiate the extraordinary. Something always shifts, because God always responds.

Divine Favor: Worship Attracts Heaven's Attention

One cannot speak of the reward of the worshipper without first addressing favor—God's unmerited kindness that rests like a banner over those who draw near to Him. King David's life was marked by divine favor, not merely because of his leadership or courage, but because he was a man after God's own heart. His songs were not performances but passionate cries of a soul in love with God. This devotion was not momentary—it was consistent.

In Psalm 5:12, David writes, *"Surely, Lord, you bless the righteous; you surround them with your favor as with a shield."* David knew this not as theory but

experience. He faced betrayal, war, shame, and even his own failures, yet God's favor never departed from him. Why? Because David continually returned to the altar of worship. When he failed, he fell into repentance through song. When he triumphed, he honored God through praise.
Likewise, Eleanor Mitchell, a fictional primary school teacher in Kentucky, lived a quiet life unknown to the world but known deeply by Heaven. Every morning before leaving for work, she would sit in her worn-out chair, open her Bible, and begin to sing softly—sometimes tearfully—songs of praise. Her classroom became a haven for children struggling with anxiety and neglect. Her colleagues noticed that wherever Eleanor went, peace followed. When the school nearly shut down due to funding cuts, a surprise grant saved it. Later, the principal—an unbeliever at the time—told her*, "I don't know what it is about you, but there's something holy around you."* Worship had attracted divine favor that overflowed to everything she touched.

Spiritual Sensitivity: Seeing Through God's Eyes
Consistent worship tunes the soul like a stringed instrument to the heart of God. The more one worships, the more attuned they become to His voice. Worship is not emotional hype; it's spiritual clarity.
In Luke 2:25-30, we meet Simeon, a devout man who waited for the consolation of Israel. Scripture says "the Holy Spirit was upon him," and he was led by the Spirit into the temple the day baby Jesus was brought in. How could he recognize the Messiah in the arms of a poor couple when so many missed it? Simeon was a worshipper. His life was one of

waiting, praying, and honoring God. Worship had refined his spiritual sensitivity to such a degree that he could perceive the eternal in the ordinary.

This sensitivity is not reserved for Bible characters. Take the fictional story of Asha Menon, a widowed grandmother in Kerala, India. After the loss of her husband, she began rising each morning to read the Psalms aloud and worship. Over time, she began to feel stirred in her spirit to intercede for neighbors or send words of encouragement. Once, she felt compelled to pray for a young mother she had only met once. That evening, she learned the woman had been contemplating suicide—but received Asha's message just in time. Worship had given Asha ears to hear and eyes to see the promptings of Heaven.

Breakthroughs in Impossible Areas

The worshipper does not strive in the flesh to unlock spiritual doors—they praise until Heaven intervenes. Breakthroughs come not through noise but through reverent obedience and exalting God above circumstances.

In 2 Chronicles 20, when King Jehoshaphat faced a vast army, he did not consult military experts first. He gathered the people, sought the Lord, and sent out worshippers. "Give thanks to the Lord, for His love endures forever," they sang. It was not strategy—it was worship. And the enemy turned on itself. God moved in response to worship.

Luis Rivera, a fictional small business owner in Colombia, struggled for years under political instability and extortion threats. Instead of compromising or falling into despair, he began to gather his employees every morning for 10 minutes of worship and prayer. One week after a particularly intense time of worship, Luis received an unexpected government clearance for his business to operate under special protection. No one could explain it—but Luis could. Worship had opened a door no man could shut.

Intimacy with God: The Ultimate Reward

The deepest reward of worship is not what happens around us, but what happens within us. Worship invites us into divine intimacy. Moses, after encountering God face to face, would descend Mount Sinai with his face glowing. His worship led to transformation, not information. The same holds true today.

Lydia Bennett, a fictional university student in London, grew up in a churchgoing family but never knew God personally. During a mission trip, she encountered a group of believers worshipping with such sincerity that she began to weep uncontrollably. That night, in her dorm room, she fell to her knees and whispered, "God, I want to know You, not just know about You." What followed was a season of awakening. She began worshipping in secret—just her guitar and her Savior—and the presence she once admired from afar became her daily portion. Worship had unlocked intimacy. Her journals overflowed with prayers, songs, and visions, not for show, but because the King had drawn near.

Emotional Healing: Beauty for Ashes

Worship is a balm for broken souls. In Isaiah 61:3, God promises *"a garment of praise instead of a spirit of despair."* Worship brings exchange—ashes for beauty, mourning for joy.

Naomi, the mother-in-law of Ruth, returned to Bethlehem saying, *"Call me Mara, because the Almighty has made my life bitter."* She had lost her husband and sons. But in the story's quiet unfolding, Ruth's faithful devotion and Boaz's redemption led to joy. Naomi held her grandson Obed in her arms—an heir in the lineage of Christ. The Scripture doesn't record Naomi singing, but her life becomes a picture of someone restored through God's redemptive plan. Worship may not always be with music—it's a posture of the heart, trusting God in deep sorrow.

Mia Tan, a fictional cancer survivor from Malaysia, had been bedridden for months after her second round of chemo. The pain was unbearable, and depression had set in. Her husband began to softly play worship music each morning. One day, Mia asked him to turn it louder. She lifted her frail arms and said, "I worship You because You're still good." That moment marked the beginning of her emotional healing. Her health improved slowly, but her soul had already risen. The spirit of heaviness had been replaced with praise.

Peace That Surpasses Understanding

Paul writes in Philippians 4:6-7, *"Do not be anxious about anything, but in every situation... with thanksgiving, present your requests to God. And the peace of God... will guard your hearts and minds."* Worship is how we practice thanksgiving. And it brings a supernatural peace that guards and anchors us.

The final story is of Jacob Green, a fictional Wall Street analyst in New York. He had all the markers of success—wealth, influence, prestige—but none of the peace. One night, overwhelmed by anxiety, he stumbled into a church service where the congregation was singing “It Is Well.” Something broke inside him. He didn’t understand everything, but he returned the next Sunday. Then the next. He began to worship at home. Anxiety didn’t vanish overnight, but peace began to rule his heart. Today, Jacob leads a small Bible study in his firm, helping others discover the peace he found—not through status, but through worship.

The Unseen but Eternal Reward

Worship is not a formula—it is a furnace, refining us, drawing us near to God. Those who worship consistently don’t just win battles—they become different people. Worship doesn’t just change circumstances; it changes identities. We become more like the One we behold. Worshippers may still face storms, losses, and valleys, but they walk through them with assurance that they are not alone—and that victory is never far, because God is always near.

The worshipper always wins—not because of what they do, but because of who they pursue.

And that, above all else, is the true reward.

Chapter 20: Living from Victory, Not for Victory

Many people spend their lives trying to earn victory—striving, battling, pushing forward, chasing after something always just out of reach. But the heart of a true worshipper beats to a different rhythm. Instead of striving for victory, the worshipper lives from victory. There is a profound difference.

Victory, for the believer, is not merely a destination or a result of hard work. It is an inheritance. It is a place we begin from, not a place we fight toward. Jesus, the Lamb who was slain and the Lion who conquered death, has already secured victory for us. Therefore, when we worship, we are not begging God to act—we are standing in agreement with what He has already done. We are aligning ourselves with Heaven's perspective. Worship isn't the path to victory. Worship is the celebration of it.

Let's unpack this truth through the lives of real people, the Word of God, and the unchanging nature of our victorious King.

Victory is the Outcome, Not the Goal

The Apostle Paul, writing from a prison cell, declared with boldness, *"But thanks be to God, who gives us the victory through our Lord Jesus Christ"* (1 Corinthians 15:57). He was not referring to the absence of conflict or suffering—Paul faced beatings, hunger, betrayal, and imprisonment. Yet he never wavered in his proclamation of victory. Why? Because to Paul, victory was already secured at the cross. His life was an offering of worship in response to that reality.

This same perspective changed the life of Daniel Okoro, a fictitious civil servant in Abuja, Nigeria. Daniel had long dreamed of building a business that would fund Christian education in rural communities. But every attempt failed. Investors pulled out, and bureaucratic delays strangled progress. At one point, his friends urged him to abandon the dream, calling it unrealistic. But Daniel, a quiet yet consistent worshipper, refused to let go. Every morning at dawn, he would kneel by his bedroom window, lift his hands, and simply say, *"Thank You for what You've already done, even if I don't see it yet."*

Two years later, an unexpected inheritance allowed him to purchase land and build the first of three schools. When asked how he stayed so hopeful, Daniel replied, *"I wasn't chasing victory. I was living from it. Worship taught me that God finishes what He starts."* Worship had realigned Daniel's vision. Victory was no longer a moving target—it was the bedrock beneath his feet.

The True Worshipper Becomes Unshakeable

The one who lives from victory does not panic in the storm. They may weep, they may stumble, but they are never crushed. Worship anchors the soul in truth and steadies the heart through every tremor of life.

Consider King Jehoshaphat in 2 Chronicles 20. When a vast army came against him, fear struck the nation. Yet Jehoshaphat didn't react with battle cries—he responded with a fast and a song. He appointed singers to go before the army, praising God for His enduring love. The result? The enemy turned on itself. Judah did not even have to lift a sword. Their worship made them unshakeable.

This is mirrored in the story of Leah White, a fictional midwife in Wellington, New Zealand. Leah's son, Jonah, was diagnosed with a rare degenerative disorder at age nine. Doctors gave him only months to live. Leah was devastated, but she made a decision: to worship through the valley.

Every night, she and Jonah would sing one hymn—sometimes barely above a whisper. Jonah passed away peacefully one morning with the words *"Jesus, I love You"* on his lips. At the funeral, Leah stood, voice trembling but strong, and said, "The enemy did not win. Jonah is healed in Heaven, and God's presence never left us." Leah didn't deny the pain—but her heart was rooted in a kingdom that cannot be shaken. Worship had made her unbreakable.

Her worship wasn't noise—it was warfare. It wasn't denial—it was defiance in the face of despair. She wasn't seeking a victory. She was standing in it.

Worshipping Through Every Season

Worship is not seasonal—it's foundational. True worshippers do not worship only in harvest or celebration. They worship in famine, in silence, in waiting. Worship becomes their language across every season of life.

The prophet Habakkuk said it beautifully: *"Though the fig tree does not bud and there are no grapes on the vines… yet I will rejoice in the Lord, I will be joyful in God my Savior"* (Habakkuk 3:17-18). Worship was not dependent on visible blessings. It was a declaration of trust in the character of God.

Reuben and Eliza Garza, a fictional farming couple in rural Argentina, understood this truth. For five years, drought devastated their crops. They sold furniture and even jewelry to pay off debts. Yet every Sunday morning, they laid out a small red cloth in the middle of their barren field and took communion together. Eliza would often say, *"We may have lost water, but we've never lost the well." In the sixth year,* rain came like never before, and their fields yielded more than any prior harvest.

The reward was not just in the restored crops. It was in the intimacy they had gained with the Lord in the dry seasons. They learned to worship in barrenness and breakthrough alike. Their praise had never been about circumstances—it had always been about the worthiness of the One they worshipped.

Living from Victory: A New Way to See

Victory is not a finish line we cross when everything finally goes right. It is the place where worship begins, because Christ has already overcome. When we truly grasp this, fear loses its grip. Anxiety gives way to peace. Control yields to trust. Worship becomes more than an event—it becomes our ecosystem.

It changes how we respond to criticism, to sickness, to uncertainty, and even to death. We no longer worship *to* feel better or *to* win a battle. We worship because we are loved, because God is faithful, because Jesus has already won. Worship is our victory song, sung long before the battle ends.

In John 16:33, Jesus says, *"In this world you will have trouble. But take heart! I have overcome the world."* He does not promise ease, but He promises victory. The worshipper clings to this—rain or shine, abundance or lack, laughter or tears.

Final Reflection

Victory is not the prize of the worshipper. It is their inheritance.

When we understand this, worship becomes breath, not effort. It becomes the natural overflow of hearts that know who they are and Whose they are. We do not need to chase what has already been won. We simply need to worship from it.

So let your life be a constant altar. Let your heart sing even when your lips cannot. Let every breath remind you that victory is not something you earn—it's something you carry.

A worshipper always wins. Not because life is always easy, but because their eyes are always fixed on the One who has already conquered all.

Amen.

Conclusion: The Final Battle is for Worship

"Then I heard every creature in heaven and on earth and under the earth and on the sea, and all that is in them, saying: 'To Him who sits on the throne and to the Lamb be praise and honor and glory and power, for ever and ever!'" – Revelation 5:13

In the end, it is not about war, wealth, or worldly success. It is about worship. The final battle is not over politics or possessions—but over who will be worshipped. From Genesis to Revelation, the undercurrent of Scripture carries one central theme: Worship belongs to God alone. And yet, throughout history, this has been the very thing contested the most.

Satan, once a glorious angel created for worship, fell because of a desire to redirect the praise meant for God to himself. This ancient rebellion echoes into every temptation, every conflict, and every distraction we face even today. The final confrontation, revealed in the book of Revelation, is not about thrones or territories but about allegiance and adoration. It's about the object of our worship.

Worship in Heaven – A Heavenly Picture (Revelation 5, 7, and 19)

In Revelation chapter 5, the scene unfolds with stunning grandeur. The Apostle John, caught up in a vision, sees a scroll that no one in heaven or earth is worthy to open. As he weeps, the elder tells him to behold the Lion of the tribe of Judah. But instead of a lion, John sees a Lamb, *"looking as if it had been slain."* The paradox is profound—the triumphant One is the sacrificed One. And the response in heaven? Worship.

The four living creatures, the twenty-four elders, and myriads of angels declare,

"Worthy is the Lamb who was slain, to receive power and wealth and wisdom and strength and honor and glory and praise!" (Revelation 5:12)

Then in Revelation 7, we see a multitude from every tribe, nation, and tongue clothed in white robes waving palm branches and shouting,

"Salvation belongs to our God who sits on the throne, and to the Lamb!"

Finally, in Revelation 19, the culmination of worship is thunderous. It is a picture of ultimate victory:

"Then I heard what sounded like a great multitude, like the roar of rushing waters and like loud peals of thunder, shouting: 'Hallelujah! For our Lord God Almighty reigns!'" (Revelation 19:6)

This is not just liturgy; it is the climactic fulfillment of all worship on earth. The heavens erupt not with a battle cry, but with a worship cry. Worship is the eternal activity of heaven. It is not a means to an end—it is the end itself.

Why Satan Fights Worship

Lucifer's fall, as described in Isaiah 14 and Ezekiel 28, wasn't due to a failure of beauty, wisdom, or function—but a corruption of heart. He said in his heart,

"I will ascend to the heavens; I will raise my throne above the stars of God… I will make myself like the Most High." (Isaiah 14:13-14)

Satan wanted the worship that belonged to God. His mission from that moment on has not changed. In the wilderness, he even dared to tempt Jesus, saying,

"All these [kingdoms of the world] I will give You, if You will fall down and worship me." (Matthew 4:9)
Jesus replied with the sword of truth:
"Away from me, Satan! For it is written: 'Worship the Lord your God, and serve Him only.'" (Matthew 4:10)
Satan knows the power of worship. It dethrones him and enthrones God. He attacks worship by:

- ✓ Distracting us with busyness and noise.
- ✓ Diluting it into performance and self-centeredness.
- ✓ Discouraging it with guilt and shame.
- ✓ Dividing it with preferences and pride.

But Jesus, our victorious Savior, taught us that worship is our weapon. He overcame temptation not through debate but through declaring truth and standing firm in worship.

Testimonies of the Final Choice
Let us consider three different lives. Their stories reflect the battles of many:
1. Lydia Ramos – The Corporate Executive
Lydia was the CEO of a global tech company. Brilliant and driven, she found her identity in her success. Though she attended church regularly, worship had become a routine obligation. It wasn't until she faced a corporate scandal—and lost everything—that her knees finally touched the floor in broken surrender. In the silence of her empty penthouse, she began to sing again—simple songs from her childhood. She said, *"When I had everything, I didn't worship. When I had nothing, I discovered that* He was everything."
Lydia's journey shows that worship is not dependent on position, but posture. In her lowest point, she discovered the highest calling—to adore her Creator.

2. Marcus Ndlovu – The Street Evangelist

In a small village on the outskirts of Johannesburg, Marcus lived and served as an evangelist. Despite poverty and persecution, he sang songs every morning with his wife and four children. When extremists burned down their gathering space, his wife wept. But Marcus lifted his hands in the ruins and declared, *"Even here, God is good. Even now, we sing."*

Eventually, that act of public worship drew the curiosity—and conviction—of some attackers, who later came to Christ. Marcus' family rebuilt not just a building, but a community of worshippers. His life proved that worship is more contagious than hate, and stronger than fear.

3. Chloe Martin – The Teen Battling Anxiety

Chloe was just sixteen when anxiety took over her life. Even in youth group, she felt invisible. One night, unable to sleep, she turned on worship music instead of her usual escape. She heard the words, *"I'm no longer a slave to fear, I am a child of God."* She began to whisper the words, then sing them. Night after night, worship became her lifeline. Her parents noticed a shift—not instant healing, but growing peace.

Chloe journaled, *"I didn't get delivered in a moment, but I was held every moment. That's worship. Not a rescue from the storm—but a hand to hold in it."*

The Worshipper Always Wins… Because God Never Loses

The final battle is for our hearts. Satan doesn't need to possess them—only distract them. But when a believer chooses to worship, even when the world shakes, heaven responds. Worship lifts us into the perspective of God's eternal throne, where victory is already secured.

To worship is to say, "You reign, even here."

To worship is to remember, "The battle is not mine, but the Lord's."

To worship is to declare, "Even if I don't see it yet, He is worthy still."

In a world warring for attention, affection, and allegiance, the worshipper stands out as a true warrior. Not with swords, but with songs. Not with fists, but with faith. And because our God is unchanging, unconquerable, and forever enthroned… the worshipper always wins.

Heaven is not far off. It's drawn near every time we lift our eyes, our voice, and our hearts in adoration. As Revelation closes, it is not with dread—but with a final chorus of worship.

"Amen. Come, Lord Jesus. The grace of the Lord Jesus be with God's people. Amen." (Revelation 22:20–21)

Let the final note of this book be the beginning of your song. Worship is not the end of your story. It is the essence of your existence. And as long as you choose to worship, you are already walking in victory.

Appendices

Appendix A: Scriptures on Worship – A Topical Index

This topical index organizes key scriptures related to worship into practical themes, making it easy for readers to find verses that align with their situation or season.

1. God Deserves Worship

- ✓ *Psalm 95:6-7* – "Come, let us bow down in worship, let us kneel before the Lord our Maker; for He is our God..."
- ✓ *Revelation 4:11* – "You are worthy, our Lord and God, to receive glory and honor and power…"
- ✓ *Exodus 20:3* – "You shall have no other gods before Me."

2. Worship in Spirit and Truth

- ✓ *John 4:23-24* – "The true worshipers will worship the Father in the Spirit and in truth..."
- ✓ *Romans 12:1* – "Present your bodies as a living sacrifice, holy and acceptable to God—this is your spiritual worship."

3. Worship in Trials

- ✓ *Habakkuk 3:17-18* – "Though the fig tree does not bud... yet I will rejoice in the Lord..."
- ✓ *Job 1:20-21* – "Then Job fell to the ground in worship and said, 'The Lord gave and the Lord has taken away; blessed be the name of the Lord.'"
- ✓ *Acts 16:25* – "About midnight Paul and Silas were praying and singing hymns to God..."

4. Worship Through Music

- ✓ *Psalm 100:2* – "Worship the Lord with gladness; come before Him with joyful songs."
- ✓ *Ephesians 5:19* – "Speak to one another with psalms, hymns, and spiritual songs..."
- ✓ *2 Chronicles 5:13-14* – When the trumpeters and singers were as one... the glory of the Lord filled the temple.

5. Worship as a Lifestyle

Colossians 3:17 – "Whatever you do... do it all in the name of the Lord Jesus..."

- ✓ *1 Corinthians 10:31* – "So whether you eat or drink or whatever you do, do it all for the glory of God."
- ✓ *Micah 6:8* – "What does the Lord require of you? To act justly, love mercy, and walk humbly with your God."

6. The Rewards of Worship

- ✓ *Psalm 22:3* – "You are holy, enthroned on the praises of Israel."
- ✓ *Isaiah 40:31* – "Those who wait on the Lord shall renew their strength..."
- ✓ *James 4:8* – "Draw near to God and He will draw near to you."

Appendix B:
Worship Playlist for Victory

This playlist includes a curated list of worship songs across generations and genres that align with the theme of victorious worship. It can be used for personal devotions, family worship, or church gatherings.

1. Songs of Victory

- ✓ "See A Victory" – Elevation Worship
- ✓ "Surrounded (Fight My Battles)" – Upper Room / Michael W. Smith
- ✓ "Champion" – Bethel Music ft. Dante Bowe
- ✓ "The Battle Belongs" – Phil Wickham

2. Songs of Surrender

- ✓ "I Surrender" – Hillsong Worship
- ✓ "Refiner" – Maverick City Music ft. Chandler Moore
- ✓ "Have My Heart" – Maverick City Music

3. Songs of Declaration

- ✓ "I Speak Jesus" – Charity Gayle
- ✓ "This Is How I Fight My Battles" – Upper Room
- ✓ "Raise a Hallelujah" – Bethel Music

4. Classic Hymns of Worship

- ✓ "It Is Well with My Soul" – Horatio Spafford
- ✓ "How Great Thou Art" – Stuart K. Hine
- ✓ "Great Is Thy Faithfulness" – Thomas Chisholm

5. Songs of Intimacy & Stillness

- ✓ "The More I Seek You" – Kari Jobe
- ✓ "In the Waiting" – David Leonard
- ✓ "I Just Want You" – Don Potter

6. Songs of Community Worship

- ✓ "Way Maker" – Sinach / Leeland
- ✓ "Goodness of God" – Bethel Music
- ✓ "King of Kings" – Hillsong Worship

Tip: *Create a personal "Worship Victory Playlist" on Spotify, YouTube, or Apple Music and keep adding songs that minister to your heart as your worship journey grows.*

Appendix C: Group Discussion Questions for Bible Study Groups

Use these questions in small groups, home fellowships, or church gatherings. They're designed to foster deep reflection, honest conversation, and practical application of the book's content.

Section I: Foundation of Worship (Chapters 1–8)

- ✓ What does worship mean to you personally? How has your understanding changed after reading this book?
- ✓ What did you learn from the biblical examples of worship? Which character's story impacted you most and why?
- ✓ How does worship reorient our perspective in times of crisis?

Section II: Identity and Transformation (Chapters 9–12)

- ✓ Have you ever wrestled with performance-driven worship? How did that impact your relationship with God?
- ✓ What steps can you take this week to shift from striving to surrender in worship?
- ✓ How has knowing your identity as a worshipper affected your confidence in prayer and spiritual authority?

Section III: Barriers and Breakthrough (Chapters 13–14)

- ✓ Which barrier to worship (pride, fear, distractions, etc.) do you most relate to?
- ✓ Describe a moment when silent worship or sacrifice brought you closer to God.
- ✓ How do you practically journal God-moments in your life? Share an example.

Section IV: Action & Lifestyle (Chapters 15–18)

- ✓ What is your biggest takeaway from the 21-Day Worship Transformation Plan?
- ✓ Share your experiences of worship at home or in your workplace. How can you grow further in those areas?
- ✓ What are your current worship goals—spiritually or practically—and how will you pursue them?

Section V: The Reward (Chapters 19–20)

- ✓ How have you seen worship produce peace, healing, or breakthrough in your life or someone else's?
- ✓ What does it mean to live from victory instead of for victory? How does worship help realign this mindset?
- ✓ In what ways can we carry this message to others—especially in difficult or secular environments?

About the Author
'GERARD ASSEY'

Gerard Assey is a Graduate in Economics, a PGD in Management (HRD) and holds a Doctorate in Leadership. Gerard holds several International Qualifications in Sales, Debt Collection, Training & Teaching, and is a 'Fellow' of the prestigious 'Institute of Sales & Marketing Management'-UK, a Certified NLP Practitioner, a 'Certified Trainer', an 'Accredited Management Teacher-Behavioral Sciences', a 'Certified Competency Facilitator', a 'Certified Management Consultant'- (the International credentials of a professional management consultant, awarded in accordance with global standards of the ICMCI); and a Certification from the University of Michigan in 'Successful Negotiation: Essential Strategies and Skills'

He is also a Member of the 'National Association of Sales Professionals' backed with several years experience in varied industries, both in India and Overseas. He also holds an 'Etiquette Consultant' Certification from the USA (by Sue Fox, Author of Best Seller: 'Business Etiquette for Dummies'. She has trained some of the top celebrities' world over). He was also a recipient of a scholarship for extensive training in Japan on 'Corporate Management for India'.

Gerard Assey is 'Founder & Chief Corporate Trainer' of the Group: '**Citius, Altius, Fortius Unlimited**'- an organization that **celebrated 20 years of Glorious Service** in 2021, focusing on 3 Core Competencies:

People. Performance. Profit; in functional areas of Sales & Marketing, HR & Organizational Development, covering Recruitment, Training & Consultancy!
Having managed organizations with large Sales Forces in India & Overseas, his specialization cover extensive areas of Sales Training (All levels - Presentation, Negotiation, Key/ Strategic Accounts Management & Managerial Skills for all sectors), Bid Proposal/ Capture Planning/ Management Trainings, Retail Sales, Customer Service & Customer Retention Programs, Training for Prevention & Collection of Debt, Self & Personal Development Programs (Time Management, Teamwork & Team Building, Business Etiquette & Personal Grooming, Leadership & Managerial Skills, People Management Skills, Train-the-Trainer etc), including preparation of Custom-designed Business Manuals for Internal (HR, Induction, and Sales etc) & External use (Instruction, User Manuals).
Gerard has successfully conducted over 6450 Trainings & Workshops (as of May '25) all across India, Middle East, Africa, Europe & S.E. Asia. Besides public programs conducted regularly, both in India & Overseas, he has some of the top names as clients whom he services from Single Owners to large Public & Government undertakings, covering all sectors, for their in-house needs.
His website: www.CollectionSkills.com is the only one in this part of the world to be featured in the 'Collections & Credit Risk Magazine-USA' under 'Who's Who in Training' and ranks TOP, along with other websites listed below on most search engines.

Gerard is author of 191 books already (May 2025), all the books being available on all online platforms and outlets as E-books and Paperbacks

A few of our business related books:

1. Bite-sized Bits on Commonsense Management
2. Heart to Heart on Life's Principles'
3. How to become a Successful Manager
4. The Sales Professionals' Master Workbook of S.Y.S.T.E.M.S
5. The Professional Business Email Etiquette Handbook & Guide
6. The Professional Business Video-Conferencing Etiquette Handbook & Guide
7. Professional Presentation Skills
8. Exceptional Customer Service
9. Professional Tele-Marketing Skills
10. Professional Debt Collection Skills
11. The G.R.E.A.T. Sales & Service Workbook
12. Sales Training Advantage for Results (*The Ultimate Sales Training Manual to enable you stand out as a S.T.A.R.*)
13. CEO Daily Planner & Organizer
14. The Sales Professionals' Master Daily Planner
15. The Professional Debt Collector's Master Daily Planner
16. My Daily Planner & Organizer
17. MY EMERGENCY INFORMATION RECORD (Family Emergency & Peace of Mind Planner)
18. The Ultimate Therapist & Counselors Planner and Organizer
19. Building an Ethical Workplace
20. Managing Relationships at Work
21. Managing Business Meetings Effectively
22. Effective Delegation Skills
23. Goal Setting for Success
24. B2B Selling by Email
25. Professional Business Etiquette & Grooming
26. Dining Etiquette & Table Manners
27. Effective Networking Skills
28. Grooming, Etiquette & Manners for Teens, Young Adults & Future Leaders
29. Inter-Personal Skills
30. Get Ready, Get Hired!
31. Selling in a Recession
32. Effective Receivables Management in an Economic Downturn!
33. Real Estate & Property Sales Training
34. Credit Sales & Accounts Receivable Management

35. Selling Skills for Real Estate & Property Advisors
36. Take G.R.E.A.T. C.A.R.E!
37. Spa, Salon & Health Club Selling Skills
38. Selling Travel, Holiday & MICE Services
39. Selling Skills for Spa's, Salons & Health Clubs
40. Retailing in Salons & Spas
41. Selling Holiday, Vacation, Tours & Packages
42. The Power of Sales Referrals
43. Selling Luxury
44. Technical Selling Skills
45. Financial Advisors Sales Training
46. Dealing with Burnout at Work Monopolize Your Markets
47. Selling to Affluent Customers
48. Growing up with Grace
49. Financial Selling Skills
50. *The Effective Manager's Guide: Key Skills to Thrive*
51. From Aspiring to Inspiring: A Guide for New Managers on the Rise
52. The Power of Focus
53. Selling with Integrity: Sell Like Jesus The Perfect Role Model!
54. 31 Habits of Champions: Your 31-Day Journey to Greatness
55. Rejecting Grasshopper Talk: From Grasshopper to Giant-Killer-*Defeating Giants Daily!*
56. Navigate the AI-Powered Future of Bid & Proposals: Up-Skill to Stay Relevant with Alternative Career Paths & Opportunities
57. Hiring Sales Winners
58. Present with Impact
59. Success Unlocked: *Breaking Free from Habits that Hold You Back*
60. Complaints to Cheers, Feedback to Gold: Mastering Complaints Management
61. Thriving Together: *Cultivating Diversity, Equity, and Inclusion*
62. Coaching Skills for Sales Managers
63. Soaring to Success in Business & Leadership: Swifter, Higher, Stronger!
64. From Classroom to Podium: A Student's Guide to Powerful Public Speaking & Presentation Skills
65. Developing Self-Discipline
66. The CEO's 31-Day Power Plan: Unlocking Success through Essential Traits

67. Credibility Matters
68. A Winning Attitude
69. Bid & Proposal Management Using AI
70. Sales Forecasting: A Practical & Proven Guide to Strategic Sales Forecasting
71. Elevate & Energize: *50 Dynamic & Fun Activities for Peak Workplace Morale*
72. 'Sales SOS! Sales on Fire! *30 Days to Conquer Chaos & the Nightmares of Success!'*
73. Mastering Sales Managerial Skills: *Building High-Performing Teams & Driving Exceptional Results*
74. Eagle-Eyed Leadership: Unleashing the Power of 31 Lessons from Eagles
75. The Ultimate Employee Training Guide: *Training Today, Leading Tomorrow*
76. Being More Accountable at Work
77. Creating a Culture of Continuous Improvement
78. Effective Questioning & Listening Skills
79. The Power of Value Selling
80. The Growth Mindset
81. Mastering Professional Help Desk Skills
82. The Power to Lead with Empathy
83. Being Prepared: The Key to Unlocking Success
84. Youthful Spark-Youth Energizers, Activities and Games-Igniting the Fun in Youth
85. Ignite your Motivation for Success
86. Elevate Your Executive Presence: *Your Roadmap to Executive Excellence*
87. Smart Decisions: *Mastering Problem Solving with Strategic Solutions for Business Success*
88. Strategic Planning: *Developing and Implementing Strategic Plans to Achieve Long-Term Business Goals*
89. The Power of Stay Interviews
90. Developing G.R.I.T.
91. Adaptability
92. Diagnosis- *A Key Skill for Leadership*
93. The Burnout-Proof Salesperson: *The Master Guide to Preventing Stress & Burnout-* Strategies for Thriving in Sales
94. Learning from Failure: *Keys to Success*
95. Customer Success Management
96. Overcoming the Killers of Motivation
97. The C-Suite Code: *Mastering Skills for Executive Excellence'*

98. Dealing with Difficult Customers
99. Unlocking Your Potential: Mastering the Top 20 Life Skills for a Brighter Future
100. Nurturing Tomorrow's Leaders: *Essential Soft Skills Every Child Must Learn*
101. Lively & Fun Party Games for Seniors & Elders
102. Role Playing for Sales Champions: From Practice to Performance
103. Fun and Exciting Party Games for Kids
104. Case Studies for Sales
105. Role-Playing for Unbeatable Customer Service
106. Case Studies in Customer Service
107. Case Studies in Winning Negotiations
108. Case Studies in Management & Leadership
109. Case Studies in Human Resources & Talent Management
110. CEO Success Blueprint: The Essential Toolkit for CEOs and C-Level Executives
111. The Salesperson's Self-Coaching Guide: *Master Your Own Self-Coaching Plan for Success*
112. Overcoming Procrastination: *Your Ultimate Guide to Stop Delaying and Start Living Your Best Life*
113. When True Colors Are Exposed: *The Journey to Unmasking Humanity*
114. Life-Changing Habits for Teens: Teen Success Blueprint for a Bright Future
115. Workplace Stress-Free: *Proven Strategies to Thrive at Work and Beyond*
116. Objection Overruled: *The Ultimate Guide to Turning 'No' into 'Yes'*
117. Building Strong Teams: *A Comprehensive Guide to Team Building*
118. Ethical & Moral Leadership in Business: *Eliminating Unethical Practices & Building a Culture of Trust & Integrity*

From the Ministry side, Gerard graduated in the very first batch of Charis Bible College-India & had for over 9 years served as a Part-time Faculty at Charis Bible College-Chennai (Andrew Wommack Ministries-Colorado, USA). He also holds a Diploma in Worship (a subject closest to his heart) from the JSOW and is also a graduate of the Advanced Mentorship Program (AMP) and the Circle Of

Ministerial Engagement (C.O.M.E.) of Prophet Jerome Fernando and a Spiritual Son of the Esteemed Prophet. An accomplished author of several Secular & Christian Books, Gerard has been on the board of a few international organizations and boasts of being the SON of the MOST HIGH GOD: An ordinary guy following an extraordinary GOD!

...And some of his most recent Christian Books being:

1. A Bouquet of Praises for My KING
2. Christian Jokes for the Serious Religious' Folks!
3. Jesus Healed You!
4. Praise24Ever! (also in Tamil version)
5. The 5G Network of GOD
6. Building Faith over F.E.A.R- FACE EVERYTHING AND RISE with JESUS
7. Hebrew and Greek Praise and Worship Words
8. Godly Mothers' and Grandmothers' Bible Story time for Kids!
9. Miracles of Jesus in Pictures
10. Raise your Praise all 365 Days
11. Thanking GOD with an Attitude of Gratitude
12. Meditating on the Attributes of GOD
13. Puppet Scripts
14. Alcohol Ruins, JESUS Reforms, Renews & Restores!
15. Habakkuk 2:2 Christian Daily Journal, Planner & Organizer
16. ABC of GOD's Word for Handwriting Practice
17. Daily Bible Verse Handwriting Practice (Building Godly Character & Faith through Cursive Handwriting Practice!)
18. Guiding Light: Fun & Faith-Building Bible Activities for Children
19. Rejecting Grasshopper Talk: From Grasshopper to Giant-Killer-*Defeating Giants Daily!*
20. Teen Titans of Faith: *Building Courage, Determination & Christ-like-Esteem*
21. I AM Empowered: *Unleashing Divine Power with Positive Declarations*
22. Be A Solution Provider-*From Passion to Purpose: A Biblical Guide to Being the Answer to the World!*
23. Miracles of JESUS
24. Parables of Jesus for a Meaningful Life!
25. A Grateful Heart: Importance of Sharing Testimonies of GOD's Grace
26. Melodies of Worship to JESUS: 31 Songs of Praise & Worship From My Heart to HIS!
27. I AM SO BLESSED!
28. My Daily Cup of Energizer

29. 31 Leadership Lessons *from* Jesus- *The Supreme Leader*
30. Peace Amidst Storms: A Biblical Guide to Conquering S.T.R.E.S.S.
31. Rise Above: 20 Biblical Eagle Lessons for Life's Triumphs
32. Godly Goal Setting: *The FAITHFUL Blueprint for a Purpose-Driven Life*
33. The Profound Attributes of our Mighty GOD: Understanding the 10S's of the Almighty
34. Worship Now, Worship Forever: *A Journey from Earthly Praise to Eternal Glory*
35. Unceasing Praise & Worship: *365 Days to Worship the King*
36. The ROAR Within: *Living with Purpose and Authority through the Power of the Holy Spirit*
37. From Potential to Purpose: Unlocking and Multiplying Your Talents & Gifts for Kingdom Impact
38. Songs from the Heart: *Worshipping GOD in Your Own Tune & Melody*
39. Awakening Praise & Worship: Hebrew & Greek Words to Raise Your Praise
40. Sing a NEW Song to the LORD Everyday: *Daily Devotions of Praise & Worship to Lift Your Heart & Glorify HIS Name*
41. *The* A.R.O.M.A. of True Worship: *Creating Worship That Delights God*
42. Becoming A Kingdom Champion: *Embracing God's Call for a Life of Purpose & Victory*
43. The Busy Businessman's Daily Devotional: 366 Crisp Truths to Start Your Day Strong
44. The Teacher's Heart: *Daily Devotions for Educators*
45. Anchored! *A 31-Day Devotional for Students Facing Life's Challenges*
46. Suddenly! Unlocking Unorthodox Breakthroughs through Unusual Worship
47. Overcoming Adversity: *Lessons from the Bible for Modern Challenges*
48. LORD, Don't do it without me
49. Kingdom Leadership: *Biblical Principles for Modern Leaders*
50. Heartprints of God- *Growing God's Way:* Daily Devotions for Kids to Shine Bright
51. Send Judah First: Let your Praises Go up First to See the Mighty Move of GOD
52. DIVINE MOMENTS: *Recognizing, Embracing, Preparing, and Walking into Life-Changing Encounters with God*
53. Be a Builder in the Kingdom: *The C.E.M.E.N.T. Guide*

to Creating a Lasting Legacy

54. Unshakable: *Pillars of Godly Womanhood* (Pillars of Faith That Changed History)
55. Lead Like a Shepherd: *14 Essential Traits for Pastoral Excellence*
56. The Worship Leader's Arsenal: *Powerful Exhortations to Ignite Thanksgiving, Praise & Worship*
57. Women of UnShakable Faith: *31-Day Devotional for Strength, Purpose & Influence*
58. Called to Teach: *A Complete 10-Week Training Guide for Impactful VBS Teachers*
59. Strumming for the KING: Cowboy Songs of Faith & Fire
60. The Ultimate Youth Camp Playbook: *50 Bible-Centered Indoor Games to Engage, Equip, and Empower Teens*
61. Glad in HIS Presence: *David's Revelation of GOD's Love & Mercy*
62. The Spirit Behind the Sound: *52 Devotionals for Worship Teams*
63. THE COWBOY'S COMPASS: *Riding the Trail of Faith with Grit & Grace*
64. Worship as My Weapon: *Living Victoriously through the Power of Praise*
65. A Worshipper Always Wins: *Living a Life of Victorious Worship*

Besides regularly contributing to business & trade journals, including international ones such as the 'Creative Training Techniques' and the 'Sales News' of the U.S.A, He is also a member of several prestigious bodies & trade associations, having participated in many Conferences & Workshops in India & Overseas.

Prior to his last assignment of leading & managing a large MNC as head, Gerard had a 3-year stint in the Middle East as a Consultant with a leading British Consultancy Firm.

As the past 'Official Country Representative' for the International Business Award- 'THE STEVIES'-(the business world's own Oscar) for about 4 years- he ensured a few Indian companies that qualify for the same every year!

Gerard can be contacted at:

Email: training@Sales-Training.in,training@CollectionSkills.com
Websites:

- www.Sales-Training.in
- www.EtiquetteWorks.in
- www.CollectionSkills.com
- www.RetailSalesTraining.in
- www.SalesTrainingIndia.com
- www.ManualPreparation.com
- www.TrainingWithPuppets.com
- www.FirstContactAcademy.com
- www.SalesAndMarketingRecruiter.com

Our TRAININGS that can help your team

- ✓ **Sales Effectiveness**: Selling Skills for any Sector: Service/ Logistics/ FMCG Realty/ Insurance & Finance/ Media/ SPA's, Health Clubs & Salons/ Key Account Management, Effective Negotiation Skills/ Bid & Proposal Management Skills/ Retail Sales Training: Any Sector (Auto, Jewelry, Clothing, Luxury etc)
- ✓ **Customer Service Skills**-Complaints Handling & Customer Retention
- ✓ **Debt Prevention & Collection Skills**
- ✓ **Etiquette & Grooming**
- ✓ **Leadership & Managerial Skills**
- ✓ **Self & Personal Development Skills**: Presentation Skills/ Effective Communication Skills/Business Proposal Writing Skills/ Problem Solving & Decision Making Skills/ Empowering Secretaries-The perfect PA! (For Secretaries & PA's)/ Effective Time Management/ Teamwork & Teambuilding/ P.R.I.D.E- **P**ersonal **R**esponsibility **I**n **D**elivering **E**xcellence

www.ingramcontent.com/pod-product-compliance
Ingram Content Group UK Ltd.
Pitfield, Milton Keynes, MK11 3LW, UK
UKHW021340190726
13845UKWH00027B/641

9 788198 697462